THE
HOMESCHOOLING
STARTER GUIDE

THE
HOMESCHOOLING
STARTER GUIDE

How to Create and Adapt
the Best Education Action Plan
for Your Needs

GINA RILEY, PHD

ROCKRIDGE
PRESS

To Ben
You will always be the one I love
most in this world. We did it—again!

Interior and Cover Designer: Linda Snorina
Art Producer: Janice Ackerman
Editor: Jed Bickman
Illustration: Courtesy of LanKogal/shutterstock.
Author photo: Courtesy of Cayla Ann Photography.

ISBN: Print 978-1-64876-513-1 | eBook 978-1-64876-514-8

R0

CONTENTS

INTRODUCTION
Map Your Way to Homeschool Success

Welcome to the incredible world of homeschooling! My name is Dr. Gina Riley, and I'll be your guide on this journey. I'm a Clinical Professor and Program Leader of Adolescent Special Education at City University of New York—Hunter College. I teach and supervise New York City public and private school teachers for most of my day and love the work so much! However, I also have more than 20 years of experience researching and practicing home education and I deeply understand the benefits, as well as challenges, involved in making the decision to homeschool. In fact, I homeschooled my own son from preschool to 12th grade. His first day of formal schooling was his first day of college! He graduated from college with a 3.96 GPA, successfully completed graduate school, and is now a writer and music educator. Most important, he is an incredible human who loves to read and learn.

Homeschooling is a form of education that grew tremendously during 2020, when I was writing this book. The percentage of families who are registered to homeschool in the United States doubled, from 5 percent to 10 percent of all families with school-age children. This percentage does not count the number of families who are home learning because of school closures or remote learning due to COVID-19. If this was the year you started thinking about homeschooling, you're in good company! Many families who started homeschooling because of COVID-19 have discovered its vast benefits and plan to keep doing it even after the pandemic ends.

In this book, we'll take a step-by-step approach so that you'll have everything you need to start homeschooling your child or teen. We'll begin by outlining the reasons homeschooling may be the right choice for you and your family. Next, we'll discuss how to create a home learning environment and develop a teaching philosophy. Then we'll explore the many homeschool models out there, so you can be informed and pick one (or a combination of a few) that works for you. We'll also talk about general standards and requirements, so you can feel confident that you're following all the rules and regulations you need to start homeschooling successfully.

Later on in the book, we'll start setting homeschool goals and making a home learning action plan. We'll also discuss how to choose a specific curriculum and create homeschool lesson plans. Additionally, we'll review what happens after that first year of homeschooling, when everyone is used to the rhythm and schedule of home learning. The most wonderful thing about homeschooling is that as you proceed, you'll notice an increase in your child's or teen's intrinsic motivation to learn. You will need to do less of the "teaching" and can relax into learning right along with your child.

Throughout the book, I'll use the term *parent* to refer to the individual or individuals responsible for the upbringing and education of the child. However, you can also homeschool as a legal guardian or grandparent. In fact, many legal guardians, grandparents, and extended family are involved in homeschooling children in their care. Also, I'll use the word *child* frequently. This refers to the child, children, teen, or teens being homeschooled in grades pre-K through 12.

Whatever your defined role is, I'm here to assure you that you're making a fantastic choice!

Homeschooling has so many benefits, and homeschool graduates have demonstrated incredible academic, social, and community-based success. I am so honored to be able to assist you in your journey. Let's start planning!

CHAPTER ONE

WHY SHOULD YOU HOMESCHOOL?

There are so many reasons homeschooling is beneficial for children and teens, including increased academic success, increased positive social behaviors, and increased civic engagement later on in life. Homeschooling also allows students to learn real-world skills right away instead of waiting until after they graduate from high school or go on to college. Many homeschooled students learn to prepare meals, do their own laundry, and assist parents or siblings with household tasks early on. Homeschooling parents themselves report many benefits of home learning for their families, including an increased intrinsic motivation to learn, improved feelings of self-confidence and self-esteem in their children, and family freedom of schedule.

You may be wondering why I chose to homeschool. In the year 2000, I was a young, single parent who was working and going to school. At first glance, homeschooling might not have seemed like a viable option for me. But I am a huge believer in the idea that homeschooling works for everyone if you want it to work. In my case, I saw my preschooler learning so many amazing things at home and through play that it seemed silly to enroll him at school when I knew I could teach him. At the time, I didn't think I would be homeschooling him for his entire school career. We just took it one year, and one step, at a time.

Why More People Are Homeschooling

There are many reasons you might be considering homeschooling for your family. Even before the COVID-19 pandemic, home education was growing as a nationwide educational movement. The number of families choosing to homeschool has grown greatly in the past decade, and homeschooling is now a popular alternative to public, private, or charter schooling.

Prior to the pandemic, researchers estimated that almost two million students in the United States were home educated, accounting for more than 3 percent of the school-age population. In 2020, that percentage increased to 10 percent, with further growth expected. Since the COVID-19 crisis began, homeschooling has grown even more rapidly than anticipated. Parents unimpressed with the remote learning provided by their local school district or concerned about the safety of mass public schooling have turned to home education in droves. I suspect that many parents will continue homeschooling after the pandemic is over, having discovered the benefits of doing so.

Parents choose homeschooling for myriad reasons. In the 1980s and 1990s, religious beliefs were the number one reason parents decided to homeschool their children, but that is not the case anymore. According to 2017 data from the National Center for Education Statistics, the top three motivations for homeschooling included concern about a child's school environment, dissatisfaction with academic instruction at school, and a desire for more faith-based education. As you can see, religious motivation is still an important and valid reason to homeschool your children, and this book is meant to help all families, both secular and religious. Other reasons parents decided to homeschool included concerns about school safety, negative peer pressure, and bullying. Approximately 12 percent of the population chose homeschooling because it better addressed their child's special needs, including physical or mental health assistance.

As homeschooling has grown, it has also become more diverse. More Black, Hispanic, and Muslim families are choosing to homeschool than ever before. These families have replaced the Eurocentric curriculum frequently seen in public schools with curricula that celebrate their unique cultures and achievements. Many military families have found home learning to be complementary to their specific needs, especially considering the frequent travel and moving that they experience. Single parent families have found ways to homeschool successfully, thanks to the growing gig economy and the increase in flexible work-from-home environments. Students who identify as

LGBTQIA+ are finding home learning to be healing, an escape from bullying and the negative attitudes they may experience in school. Homeschooling is the perfect environment to address a student's unique learning and social-emotional needs, whether that child is a 5-year-old kindergartner or a 17-year-old high school senior.

Key Factors to Consider Before Homeschooling

Homeschooling is wonderful because it allows children to engage in learning activities that utilize their strengths, interests, and preferences. In a homeschooled environment, children and teens get one-on-one attention, and lessons are individualized. Many homeschooling families appreciate the freedom of schedule that homeschooling brings them, as they are no longer at the mercy of the school calendar or school day. Learning can happen at any time, giving students and parents the freedom to schedule their day, their week, and their school year in the way that works best for them.

There are, however, challenges to the home learning environment. Homeschoolers don't have immediate access to peers within a classroom structure, so social gatherings may sometimes have to be intentionally planned. Homeschoolers also may not have the benefit of having a gymnasium space to engage in athletic activities or music or art rooms to engage in creative activities. That leaves the creation of these spaces to the parent, with some help from their child. In a home learning environment, the parent is the facilitator of a child's education, and therefore has a lot more work and responsibility than most parents do, because they have to manage not only their child's well-being, but also their child's education.

Time Commitment

Homeschooling does take a rather large time commitment. If a family decides to engage in more formal methods of homeschooling, they must choose and/or purchase a curriculum and plan individualized lessons. They must grade and comment on papers and tests. If students are going to be engaged in more project-based or informal homeschooling, parents need to pave the way for participation in activities and field trips. Each state has regulations regarding home learning, and so whatever method parents choose, they have to complete quarterly paperwork for their local district. This paperwork may include attendance reports, subject-based learning summaries, and individual student progress assessments. Parents also have to create and manage student schedules, although the children can help with this.

However, it's important to note that even when a child goes to a traditional school, parents still have to attend to many of these same tasks. Parents provide homework help and schedule their child's activities. Schools send home paperwork to be read and signed. Parents transport their children to and from activities. The difference is that in homeschooling, a parent has to be able to take on the main responsibilities of managing everything that would be the job of a teacher or staff member at a conventional school.

Financial Impact

Families who have homeschooled point out that home learning does have an impact on their finances. Because parents need to be at home more to facilitate their child's learning, families may need to change their work schedules to create a lifestyle conducive to home education. This change in work or scheduling sometimes leads to a reduction in overall income. Parents must buy curricula, supplies, and subscriptions and create opportunities for local travel. This can add up and have an impact on budgets.

However, there are ways around the loss of income. Because of changes in work culture, homeschooling is more accessible to everyone in many ways. In today's work-at-home and gig economy, parents can create income and homeschool at the same time. More single parents and lower income families than ever before are choosing to homeschool. Remember that homeschooling can also be an extended family affair, with grandparents, friends, and neighbors all pitching in to help, if that's available to your family.

Socialization

People without direct experience of homeschooling are typically the ones most concerned with the socialization of homeschoolers. This may be because within the more traditional school-based culture, socialization is seen as something that happens primarily in school. Media stereotypes and outside observers raise concerns about homeschoolers being socially isolated and not part of more formal institutionalized social groups. Yet homeschoolers themselves report they have good social lives from being involved in activities like dance, theater, music, sports, and Boy Scouts/Girl Scouts. Some researchers have even postulated that homeschoolers may be better socialized than their schooled peers because of more positive, age-mixed, and real-world social interactions. A study by educational researcher Joseph Murphy showed that homeschoolers performed as well as, and sometimes better than, their private- and public-school counterparts in measures of socialization. And a study by Richard Medlin of homeschooled students' social skills reported that homeschooled students tend to be more cooperative, assertive, empathetic, and self-controlled than public school children and called homeschooled students' social skills "exceptional."

That being said, homeschool parents do have to take an active role in creating social opportunities for their children. They can easily accomplish this by enrolling children in art, music, theater, dance, or sports-based lessons or by having children become involved in community programs such as Boy Scouts, Girl Scouts, 4H, or Boys and Girls Clubs. Churches, synagogues, mosques, and other faith-based organizations can also assist in creating a sense of community for homeschooled students. When I was homeschooling my son, the local homeschool group provided countless social activities he was able to take part in. In fact, most of our homeschooling was done outside the home, in the company of other homeschooling families. We would explore museums, state parks, historic houses, and playgrounds together. For lunch or at the end of the day, we would all sit together and have a picnic or potluck meal.

Household Management

When a family chooses homeschooling, their home or apartment becomes more than a place to relax, eat, and socialize; it also becomes a place to learn and grow. Therefore, some homeschooling parents may need to create a space specifically for home learning, which may mean reorganizing a part of a room or an entire room. If that is not possible, parents can create homeschooling nooks in other rooms for their child or children.

For example, the kitchen table is a cooking and eating space, but it can also be a place to create art. The living room can not only become a space to relax and watch television, but also a place to keep books, toys, and musical instruments. Many homeschooling parents use their bathrooms to accommodate scientific experiments, confining a messy project to a bathtub, shower space, or sink.

One of the benefits of home learning is that students see what's going on in their home on a daily basis, and so can become more responsible for the space, too. Just like a teacher may ask students to help clear or clean a classroom space, a parent can ask a home learner to do the same with their work space or spaces throughout the house. Homeschoolers can learn the tasks needed to manage a household quickly and efficiently, and these tasks are all part of learning how to be a functioning adult.

Resources

Homeschooling families are in charge of the cost of the resources they use, and microscopes, textbooks, notebooks, computers, and subscriptions can become costly. That is why it's important to create and stick to a budget for home learning. However, there are tricks that many homeschooling parents use to keep their home learning budget low. Here are a few:

» School supplies can be purchased in August, when many of the big-box office supply stores have major sales.

» If you choose to use a formal curriculum, get in touch with a homeschool support group near you to see if they host a curriculum swap each year. (Try a quick online search for groups near where you live.) Many homeschooling groups hold curriculum swaps or sales where families sell their used textbooks and supplies for low prices.

» If you're purchasing any tech items or books from a book retailer, explain that you are a homeschooling family and ask if they give an educator's discount. (Many retailers offer this!)

» Utilize your local library for books, magazines, news-papers, and free or low-cost workshops for adults, kids, and teens. Some homeschooling families use their local libraries as self-directed learning centers and resource places.

» Take advantage of free days at museums, historic houses, monuments, and zoos that otherwise charge an entrance fee. If there's someplace you visit frequently, consider purchasing an annual membership so that you have unlimited access to it throughout the year. (When I was homeschooling my son, we purchased a member-ship to a different place each year, allowing us to spend a year's "residency" at a museum or historic house we loved.)

» Use your taxpayer money well! Many town or city highway departments, sanitation centers, or water companies will give a free tour of their facilities to taxpayers once a year.

» Get active at local and state parks. Local parks provide playground equipment you may not have access to at home, and state parks allow individuals to roam freely on the land and engage in many wonderful activities.

Now that you have an overview of what you're signing up for, let's get started on your homeschooling journey. The first step to setting up your homeschool is to make your home into a learning environment. We'll tackle this in the next chapter.

CHAPTER TWO

CREATE THE BEST LEARNING ENVIRONMENT FOR YOUR HOME

When I was a young, poor single mother, I homeschooled my son in the basement of the house we lived in. I created a playroom out of our main living space, as we didn't have a formal living room. This playroom housed our building bricks, board games, toy bins, and craft items. We had a desk with a computer. There was a small sofa we used for reading or playing. We conducted science experiments in the sink of a small bathroom or in the laundry room. The bedroom housed books, projects my son had created, and a bed. We shared a kitchen with my family upstairs, so the kitchen provided a communal space where we would gather together to cook and eat meals. The outdoors became an extension of our learning environment, and outside was where we'd run, play, and take walks together. Libraries and parks became our second home, and we would take field trips to museums and zoos in the city or historic houses nearby. Because we lived in such a small space, the world became our classroom, as did the people inside that world. We knew our grocer, the bank teller, our postman, and our repair people; and we knew all of them well. Our next-door neighbor became my son's best friend, and they spent many hours together repairing a Ford Model T and working on toy train sets. The size of your space does not matter. What matters is the environment you create for your child. This learning environment can, and should, extend outside the four walls of your home or apartment.

Why Your Learning Space Is Important

A dedicated learning space for your children or teens at home can drive creativity, sharpen focus, and ignite their passion to engage with their academics, as well as with the world around them. The size of the space doesn't matter. It is the overall environment of the home that matters. Spaces are physical, but they're also mental and emotional.

If you live in a small apartment, a learning space can be as small as a corner of a room. Engage your child in thinking about what that corner may look like. Perhaps it has a desk and chair, but maybe it also has a small couch or reclining chair to read and do work on. If you live in a house, this space may be an entire room or part of a room. What matters is that your child is involved in providing a vision for the space. After all, they are the one who's going to work in that space.

Space also has a big psychological impact. Your child's primary workspace should be quiet and peaceful. It should be a place where a child or teen can work and think and be curious and creative. It should not be a space where family drama occurs or where a child can hear parents arguing. One benefit of a public, private, or charter school is that it's separate from the home. So if a child lives in a home filled with conflict, they are somewhat shielded from that conflict during the day. A home learning environment, on the other hand, forces families to work together to create an optimum environment for their child.

It's also essential to develop a space where a child can feel intrinsically motivated to engage in schoolwork and interests. Research by psychologists Edward Deci and Richard Ryan tells us that there are ways we can create an environment that's conducive to increasing a learner's internal motivation. Parents must help foster three attributes in their kids: a sense of competence, a sense of autonomy, and a sense of relatedness.

Competence: Children and teens need to live and grow in an environment that acknowledges their individual strengths. They also need positive, specific praise that reflects those strengths. So if a child enjoys and is good at writing, it's important for parents to acknowledge and support that strength in every way they can. This can be done by utilizing competence-based language. For example, "Wow! That was a beautiful sentence you wrote. The way you used language to describe that scene was amazing."

Autonomy: Children and teens need to have choice and freedom within their everyday lives. If a child wants to play in the morning and work on their schoolwork in the afternoon, parents need to respect and acknowledge that choice. If a teen prefers to do math late at night, that choice should also be respected. Students need to learn how to shape and schedule their own day so that it works for them. Of course, parents have a schedule they need to work with, too, so the key is to collaborate with your child on a daily or weekly schedule that works for everyone.

Relatedness: Children and teens need to know that no matter what they decide, they are unconditionally loved and accepted by their parents or guardians. Unconditional love and acceptance allows students the freedom to take risks and make mistakes, knowing that someone has their back no matter what. It also allows students the opportunity to make their own decisions throughout their lives.

Providing physical, mental, and emotional space for intrinsic motivation to flourish leads to enhanced positive outcomes in children, including increased academic success, increased social-emotional learning, and enhanced productivity. It's important to provide physical space where your child can learn. However, creating an overall learning environment that allows for academic achievement, self-confidence, and self-determination is the most important gift you can give your child for later success in life.

How to Map Out Your Learning Space

Of course, we would all love to have an entire room within our house or apartment that could serve as a home classroom for our children. But we all live in different-sized spaces, and sometimes it's not possible to have a room dedicated for learning. A homeschool space does not have to be large or fancy. All it must offer is an environment conducive to learning.

Give Your Space a Purpose

Whatever size space you dedicate to home learning, it has to have a purpose. To have a purpose, it has to contain the needed supplies to work productively. For example, if a learning space is the corner of a dining room table, that space should hold writing utensils, notebooks, textbooks, art materials, and digital devices. The area should be designed by the child so they can take ownership of the space to make it their own. Perhaps they would like to decorate the space with colorful artwork they've created or with motivational posters. Maybe they would like to give the space a theme, like planets, travel, or music.

If you're lucky enough to have a whole room to dedicate to home learning, let your child choose the paint color and furniture for that room. I have one friend whose daughter chose a green, pink, and gold theme for a room, and she loved it so much that she decided she wanted to study interior design. Having kids help design their spot for learning is a great way to increase intrinsic motivation to learn and study!

Keep It Quiet

Make sure the home learning space you and your child choose is a quiet spot—an escape from family distraction and noise. The quieter the space is, the more focused and engaged your child will be. A quiet space is especially important for students with attention-deficit/hyperactivity disorder (ADHD) or autism, or for a child who is more introverted or extremely sensitive. Optimal acoustic conditions, according to research, are important for enhanced learning. The best environment for home learning is a space free from chatter, phone calls, television, and intense family discussions. That being said, some students prefer to work with music or dull noise in the background. This sound preference should be honored. For those students, listening to music (especially classical or jazz music) can be motivating and assist with absorption of material. They can also use headphones to create a focused environment when acoustics in a room are not ideal. A computer with a comfortable headset is a wise investment for home learning success, allowing students to think, learn, and grow in optimal acoustic surroundings.

Make Sure You Get Enough Light

Many education experts say that a clear, well-lit place is the most effective learning space. The right lighting can make a person happier and more productive. Therefore, when creating a home learning room or corner, you want to make sure that the space is well lit. Natural light is best; it can increase your child's productivity, alertness, and attention. In fact, a study published in *Scientific American* on the relationship between light and activity demonstrated that students who were exposed to more sunlight had higher reading and math results than children in less sunny environments. However, if natural light is unavailable, the light from lamps or ceiling lights will do. Design experts will state that layered light is the best light. This means there should be multiple light sources in varied spaces throughout a room. As an example, a room may contain light from a ceiling fixture, a larger floor lamp on the side of the room, and a small tabletop lamp. A 60- to 80-watt halogen bulb creates the most relaxing light, and LED bulbs are also environmentally friendly and create a peaceful light source. Interestingly, fluorescent lighting, found in most schools and offices, emits harsh light that can strain eyes and increase fatigue. Some children love the glow of string lights (the kind often seen during holidays), so feel free to use them year-round in your child's learning space. They make learning fun!

Give Your Child Ownership

Ownership of their learning is one of the most important gifts you can give your child. Children need to know that learning is not something that happens only within the hours of 8 a.m. and 3 p.m., Monday through Friday, at school. Instead, learning happens every day and everywhere. This is why it's so important that your child be involved in creating a learning space just for them. Through the activities of creating their own space, they learn measurement, geometry, architecture, and elements of interior design. They also gain a sense of competence, the feeling of knowing that they are good at things and can accomplish anything they set their mind to. The learning space the child designs should feel like them, and should contain their favorite artwork, signs, decorations, blankets, and items. That way, when a parent arrives to facilitate an assignment or a reading, they are getting invited into the child's own space. This also means that the child becomes the one in charge of the cleanliness and organization of their learning space, and they begin to learn that when their space is tidy, their overall life feels more organized, too. This feeling may extend to other areas of the home as well, and you may be surprised by how many times your child assists (without being asked) with cleaning and organizing the kitchen, the bathroom, and other spaces in your home or apartment.

Use What You Have

Remember, I was a single mom with multiple responsibilities for the first six years my son and I were homeschooling. We had very little in terms of space and only a tiny amount of money for a homeschooling budget. So everything we did used everyday materials we already had at home, and we purchased any supplies or furniture we didn't already have at secondhand shops or garage sales.

A coffee table in our house was transformed into a desk, and later, into our "general store" where my child learned math by "selling" items and creating receipts for visitors to our home. We stored our playthings and learning materials in plastic bins or painted toy boxes made from cardboard shipping and appliance boxes. Our sofa had a pullout bed for reading and playing. The outdoors became our second home, and we spent hours playing and learning about rocks, trees, plants, and the weather.

Homeschooling really doesn't require a lot of money. Everything you need, you can buy used, and most necessary community resources (such as the library and park) are free. All you need to homeschool is a willing heart and mind, and the motivation to facilitate your child's educational journey. It also helps to set your intentions about *how* you want your child to learn, and that's what we'll explore in the next chapter.

CHAPTER THREE

DEVELOP YOUR OWN TEACHING PHILOSOPHY

When I started homeschooling, all I knew was that I wanted to retain my child's innate curiosity and intrinsic motivation to learn. I saw how much he loved learning and loved the world, and I didn't want to take that away from him. He didn't even know what an A+ on a report card felt like, yet he wanted to master the identification of rocks and minerals. I wanted him to always have that feeling of competence and self-satisfaction.

However, that goal was very different from the one I grew up with. My mother was a guidance counselor at a public school, and my father was a mail carrier who also worked in afterschool programs and community centers teaching children about writing and stamp collecting. My father was an orphan and saw school as the key to a successful life. My mother was the first in her family to get a bachelor's degree and, later, a master's degree. Academic achievement was of utmost importance in our family, and they were worried about their grandson who "didn't go to school," especially since we lived in an area with a high-ranking school district.

But I knew that this was the right path for my child, and I did what I thought was best.

I had to "deschool" myself and get rid of ingrained and societal expectations regarding schooling and learning. Growing up, I was always the nice girl who got good grades, and I had wonderful (and awful) teachers who shaped my educational journey. Did I remember or absorb most of what I learned? Nope. I studied to do well on tests and handed in creative projects to impress my teachers. I wanted the A and didn't really care about anything else. I was totally extrinsically motivated, and I excelled because of the praise or good grade I would get at the end of a school quarter.

Homeschooling my son made me rethink everything I'd thought about schooling, learning, and teaching. Most of all, it gave my son the confidence to be whoever he wanted and to live his life through his own self-determined and self-directed expectations. Intrinsic motivation, for us, was the greatest gift of homeschooling. Now, intrinsic motivation in learning is the focus of my work, writing, and research as a professor of education.

Comparisons of Major Education Philosophies

One of the most helpful things you can do as you begin your own homeschooling journey is to think about your teaching philosophy. A teaching philosophy is made up of core educational beliefs that will guide you on your home learning journey. In schools of education across the country, teacher candidates write out their teaching philosophy in order to solidify the teaching and learning beliefs they want to apply to their own classroom. Contemplating the teaching philosophy that you most identify with is a great first step in your homeschooling journey.

Perennialism

Perennialism is an educational philosophy that focuses on the teaching and learning of classic ideas that have endured over many generations. Perennialism, also called *classical education*, concentrates on the study of great works of literature from the finest thinkers, such as Homer, Sophocles, Vyasa, Plato, Aristotle, Lao Tsu, Augustine, Hafez, Chaucer, Shakespeare, Tagore, Milton, Austen, Melville, Rumi, Freud, and Faulkner. The main goal of perennialism is to teach students how to think critically and analytically over time in a quest for knowledge and truth.

CORE VALUES

Adopters of perennialism will concentrate on teaching the core subjects of reading, writing, math, history, and science. This form of classic education takes much effort and planning, and students learn major subjects sequentially, from basics to more advanced topics, from the beginning of historical and scientific thought until the present time. For example, students may learn about Greek gods and simultaneously do a historical study of ancient Greece. This study may conclude with reading, comprehending, and analyzing Homer's *The Iliad* and *The Odyssey.*

HOW TO APPLY IT

Perennialism is highly discussion-based, and parents who adopt this philosophy must be open to relearning basics and rereading the classic books they assign to their child. Parents who adopt perennialism as a core educational philosophy must be prepared to do a lot of direct teaching and analyzing of texts with their child. This is a rigorous and systematic philosophy.

PROS AND CONS

The wonderful thing about this teaching philosophy is that it is low-tech and inexpensive. You can find many of the classic perennialist texts free at a local library or even online through Project Gutenberg (ProjectGutenberg.org). You can also find great, very-low-cost paperback books at local book stores, and parents can piece together a rich, classic curriculum for less than $100 a year. A classic book or perennialist curriculum is text-heavy though, and it may not be appropriate for students with certain special needs.

YOU MIGHT ADOPT THIS PHILOSOPHY IF . . .

You might adopt this philosophy if you and your child enjoy classic literature or feel comfortable with a Charlotte Mason–type curriculum (see page 37) or classical homeschooling philosophy (see page 35). Many faith-based homeschoolers also adopt perennialism as a philosophy because of its focus on analyzing books written by famous saints and theologians, as well as the Bible. Parents of gifted and talented students may enjoy the analytical nature of perennialism, and those who want to provide their children with a multicultural education can find so many incredible classic books by authors of color and authors from other cultures.

Essentialism

Essentialism is an educational philosophy focused on the teaching and learning of core subjects and basic skills. William C. Bagley, an American educator, was considered the father of essentialism, and he wrote about the importance of subject-based learning and direct teaching.

CORE VALUES

Essentialism focuses on grade-based, conceptual learning. Subjects are *scaffolded*. This means students start with simpler topics and ideas and gradually move on to more difficult concepts. Scaffolding may also be helpful when homeschooling students with special needs and/or linguistic needs. Essentialist philosophy is commonly used in US public schools, where a specific time (a school period) focuses on a specific subject. When state or county officials think of homeschooling, most are thinking of parents using an essentialist philosophy.

HOW TO APPLY IT

More-traditional homeschoolers are essentialists. They usually follow a subject-based time schedule, which is similar each day. For example, they may start with learning math in the morning and then move on to an hour each of history, science, and English language arts. Afternoons are for more project-based learning or enrichment activities. Parents use this schedule each day throughout the year. Essentialists also depend on direct instruction and lecturing, where the parent instructs the child on a specific subject or topic, and the student takes notes. Assessments through projects, quizzes, or tests are an important part of essentialism, and the use of these assessments helps show the student's mastery and their ability to successfully move forward from a concept or topic.

PROS AND CONS

Essentialism is teacher-centered and tends to be low-tech. Learning is dispersed through textbook learning and worksheets, and parents create lesson plans for each subject, every day. Learners with disabilities, first-time homeschoolers, and non-native English speakers sometimes thrive under the structure essentialism provides, as it replicates the learning that happens within a public school classroom.

YOU MIGHT ADOPT THIS PHILOSOPHY IF . . .

You might adopt this philosophy if the focus on scaffolding concepts would be helpful when homeschooling a child with special learning and/or linguistic needs. Many faith-based homeschoolers also practice essentialism, enjoying its traditional and organized structure. However, those homeschoolers who are looking for something different than a traditional classroom structure replicated at home may feel stifled by the essentialist philosophy.

Romanticism

Romanticism is an educational philosophy that relies on intuition to teach emotional self-awareness. Romanticism was popular during the Age of Enlightenment (18th century) and focuses on self-awareness and the inherent goodness of humanity as a way to improve people, the self, and society as a whole. Jean-Jacques Rousseau (1712–1788), philosopher, composer, and author of *Emile*, a book about a boy who was homeschooled by his tutor, is the best-known romanticist. Rousseau also wrote *The Confessions of John-Jacques Rousseau* (1782), in which he discusses his own educational journey.

CORE VALUES

The goal of the romanticist philosophy is to empower students to fulfill their own educational needs. They do this by utilizing the traits of imagination, intuition, individuality, idealism, and inspiration: the five I's of romanticism.

HOW TO APPLY IT

Students are taught through a self-directed learning stance; they decide what they want to learn and take responsibility for their own education. Those who follow the romanticist philosophy are also generally *unschoolers*, or individuals who learn through real-world experiences that generally fit their strengths, interests, and individual needs. Unschooling is the opposite of "school at home." In unschooling, there are no assignments, no set curriculum, and no structured assessments. Within an unschooling environment, parents do not directly teach or provide direct instruction. Instead, they provide an environmental context that supports their child's learning and development. Older unschoolers may take on apprenticeships and other volunteer or paid work experiences to supplement their learning.

Those who adhere to a romanticist philosophy believe strongly in student-led learning. If a child or teen enjoys utilizing technology, romanticism can be very high-tech in nature. However, if a student prefers a more traditional approach, technology does not have to be used. Romanticism is an effective option for students with special needs, as a key feature of this philosophy is adapting and differentiating curriculum for students with disabilities. Working parents who don't have a lot of time to create lesson plans may also appreciate this student-directed philosophy, as the student creates their own day.

YOU MIGHT ADOPT THIS PHILOSOPHY IF . . .

You might adopt this philosophy if you're intrigued by self-determined, self-directed learning, or unschooling. Gifted and high-achieving students may also find this philosophy attractive because it allows them to explore, in great depth, topics that interest and intrigue them. Older homeschooled teens tend to enjoy this type of learning because of its focus on work, volunteer, and internship opportunities. It's also similar to a college environment in which students get to choose their own classes and curriculum.

Progressivism

Progressivism is a philosophy rooted in the idea that progress and change are essential to educational success. The main goal of progressivism is to teach students how to develop an individualized approach to task management, problem-solving, and the overcoming of challenges. Within progressivism, education must be personalized to be meaningful.

CORE VALUES

John Dewey (1859-1952), American psychologist, philosopher, and academic, was one of the most significant voices of the progressivist philosophy. One of his most famous quotes, found in his work *My Pedagogic Creed*, states, "The child's own instincts and powers furnish the material and give the starting point for all education." Dewey had a strong belief in the intrinsic motivation of the learner, outside of traditional school. In his 1916 work, *Democracy in Education*, he also says "the very process of living together educates." He means that living and learning cannot be separated—something homeschoolers know and experience every day of their lives.

HOW TO APPLY IT

Those who homeschool using a progressivist philosophy focus on the abilities, strengths, and interests of their child. The learning of core subjects like math, science, English language arts, and history is done through group activities and cooperative learning activities, either with fellow homeschoolers or the family unit. Thanks to social media, homeschooled students from different places can decide to link up and work together on a specific project. Progressivists believe strongly in the power of experimentation, or trying out learning within real-world contexts, as well as the importance of questioning what one has learned through discussion and conversation.

PROS AND CONS

Progressivism is student-centered, and can be done in a high- or low-tech way. It's truly a learning philosophy that works for all. Parents of students with special needs may be particularly attracted to the hands-on aspect of progressivist learning, which adheres to Universal Design for Learning standards and assists with students' audio, visual, and kinesthetic learning needs. (The Universal Design for Learning is a framework used by educators and homeschooling parents to create learning environments that take into consideration individual learning differences.) Although parents are needed for discussion, conversation, and facilitation, progressivist learning puts education in the hands of the learners themselves.

Because of its visionary nature, progressivist philosophy works well for students who are gifted and talented, and/or can think outside the box. Its tactile focus also allows students who are multicultural and multilingual to experience learning and the world in a unique way.

YOU MIGHT ADOPT THIS PHILOSOPHY IF . . .

You might adopt this philosophy, and its focus on collaboration and group work, because progressivist learning can be done well within homeschool groups and learning pods. Those who have sought homeschooling to create educational change within their families or community will appreciate the progressivist philosophy.

Write Your Own Education Philosophy Statement

An education philosophy statement is a purposeful and reflective essay that breaks down a teacher's beliefs and practices. This statement becomes a helpful tool to begin with at the start of the school year and to look back on at the middle and end of the school year to see how your philosophy and ideas have changed once you've put them into practice. Most educational philosophy statements are around 300 words (one double-spaced page) and are written in the first person (for example, starting with "I believe . . ."). Statements have an introduction, body, and conclusion, and address such topics as the definition of education and learning, teaching expectations, and what the parent will do to create a positive learning environment for their child.

EXAMPLE Education Philosophy Statements

Here's an example of an educational philosophy written by a parent of a child with disabilities:

> My mission in life is to help my child achieve academic success and grow as an individual. As a home educator, I'll create engaging instruction and activities. I strongly believe it's important to modify my teaching style in order to help my child grow in all ways—academically, socially, and emotionally. When working with my daughter, I'll work to meet all of her needs in order to help her realize her full potential. Through my own experiences as a learner and teacher, I've seen that children who get individualized attention and care can grow into successful young adults who can make a difference in the world.
>
> The way I will meet my daughter's needs is by creating adapted lessons that meet her individual learning style. I'll show videos so that she'll be able to visualize a topic. I'll explain difficult vocabulary to her and use visuals to explain the definitions. I'll give my daughter the opportunity to work with homeschooled peers. This will allow for group discussion and new ideas to be expressed. To make my lessons engaging,

I'll use my daughter's interests. I'll check on any topic my daughter struggles with. I will scaffold anything that needs review, going back to simpler concepts and then moving toward more complex ones. For example, if my daughter is struggling with multiplication of integers, as a scaffolding tool, I'll give her a printed multiplication table to utilize.

I'll support my daughter to correct any misconceptions she has. I'll create study guides and review sheets that go over important vocabulary, mathematical equations, and steps to solving a problem. This will help my daughter feel prepared for assessments. As a home educator, I'll create lessons that will challenge my daughter to become a problem solver and thinker. When my daughter walks into her learning space to work, she'll feel a supportive, positive, and thought-provoking environment.

In this essay, you'll find that the parent adheres to the philosophies of essentialism and progressivism. She's dedicated to teaching her child according to the child's interests, strengths, and needs. She also believes strongly in scaffolding and adapting learning materials to her child's needs and learning preferences. The parent ends the statement by expressing what she plans to do within the home learning environment, and how she wants her daughter to feel when entering her learning space.

This example of an educational philosophy is written by a parent with multiple children:

I believe that learning happens through play and exploration with the environment at all ages (not just the childhood years). In our home learning environment, I want fun and learning to go together. I'll provide my children with books, arts-and-crafts supplies, and technology, as needed. We'll go on walks to explore our neighborhood and take lots of field trips to explore the world outside our town. I also want my children to see that work and play go hand-in-hand. My children will see me work, and I'll assist them and facilitate their work.

Trips to the grocery store will help with basic math skills. My children will be involved in household budgeting. They'll know how to change a tire and check oil in a car. They'll learn skills such as cooking, gardening, and cleaning at home. Home will be an extension of our learning environment.

As my children grow, I want them to take advantage of internships and apprenticeships, as well as volunteer opportunities in areas that interest them. My youngest child already loves animals and has asked to walk dogs at the local animal shelter. I'll facilitate by calling the shelter so he can do this. He says he wants to be a veterinarian. He knows his future is unlimited. All my children do.

I want their life to be filled with joy. I want them to see school and the learning we do as an extension of that joy and not separate from it. I don't mind a messy home if people are happy. (We can all help each other tidy up at the end of the day). Essentially, I want my children to love learning and to see life as learning.

In this essay, you see clear evidence of the parent adhering to the progressivist and romanticist philosophies. Progressivism is seen especially in the parent's plans to help make possible a real-world experience that honors his son's love for animals.

Romanticism is evident in the parent's emphasis on celebrating individual interests, his mention of volunteer work and apprenticeships, and his focus on facilitating his children's intrinsic motivation for learning.

Overall, writing an education philosophy statement is a fantastic way to solidify your beliefs about learning before you begin your home education journey. All it takes is a pen and paper or a computer, and an hour of time. Once you complete your statement, you can ask older children and teens to write one, too. You may be surprised by what they come up with!

Now that you've learned about educational philosophies and are on the path to developing your own, the next step is to explore homeschool models. That's what we'll do in chapter 4.

CHAPTER FOUR

PICK THE BEST HOMESCHOOL MODEL FOR YOUR NEEDS

We can define a *homeschool model* as the specific method or methods you'll use to actually teach your child. In this chapter, we'll compare several models to discover what they are and how to use them so you can evaluate which is the best fit for your homeschooling family.

Some parents prefer to model their homeschooling on traditional school, while others want to take a hands-off approach. When I started homeschooling my son, I knew I didn't want to replicate the traditional classroom; how-ever, I did want him to gain some school-based skills, like reading and math. The state we homeschooled in—New York—had more stringent requirements than other states, and so we had to choose a curriculum. Our homeschooling tended to be eclectic—that is, a mix of several models. I purchased a Waldorf-based curriculum, since it had some classical influences, as well as a focus on creativity and exploration of the natural world. We used the curriculum lightly, reviewing required books and content a couple of times a year. But most of the time, we unschooled—a form of learning through life, which we'll discuss again later in this chapter. Unschooling gave my son the freedom to focus on his strengths and interests, while the Waldorf curriculum provided a grounding in the topics he needed to know within a specific grade level.

The homeschool model you choose has to be a good fit for your family and, most of all, a good fit for the child or children you're homeschooling. If you choose a classical model, for example, you're going to need to schedule some time to do reading and lesson planning each week, and your child is going to need dedicated schoolwork time each week. An unschooling model, on the other hand, provides more flexibility and less official pre-planning, and your child can have the freedom to choose where, when, and how to work on projects of interest.

Comparisons of Major Homeschool Models

A homeschool model is a blueprint that helps you build a framework for the specific learning strategies and methods you will use to reach your child's educational goals. Homeschool models also become tools to figure out the curriculum, supplies, and resources you may need to start homeschooling for the year. In this section, we'll review seven homeschool models.

The Classical Method

The classical method of homeschooling centers on providing students with a liberal arts education focused on ancient Roman and Greek teachings, as well as a steady diet of classic books, also known as the great books. Core elements of this method include the learning of Latin and logic, as well as using chronologically sequenced instruction in major subject areas such as English language arts, math, science, and history. Faith-based homeschoolers may use the classical method to teach biblical ideas and to study Greek and Latin. The main goal of the classical approach is to foster skills of critical, independent, and analytical thinking.

Classical education uses a *trivium model*, a system in which children go through three main stages of learning as they grow and develop. At the grammar stage, foundational skills are taught with a focus on memorization and repetition. During the logic stage, the emphasis is on asking relevant questions and building on prior knowledge and teachings. The rhetoric stage then builds on the previous stages. Students learn persuasive essay writing and debate skills at this stage, and they review the intricacies of politics, economics, and world events. The goal is for teens at this stage to think and develop opinions for themselves.

CORE CONCEPTS

Within a classical education, curriculum is based on classic books and lessons. Susan Wise Bauer and Jesse Wise's book *The Well-Trained Mind: A Guide to Classical Education* is a critical resource. As a child gets older, the Socratic method is used to explore and debate ideas. Socratic conversations allow students in the logic and rhetoric stages to ask relevant questions, think critically, and come to conclusions about a particular topic or realm of knowledge.

HOW TO IMPLEMENT THIS MODEL

How classical education is implemented depends on the specific subject being taught. For example, during an English language arts lesson at the grammar stage, children may begin to learn to read and grow in their knowledge of sentence, paragraph, and grammatical structure. During the logic stage, students may expand their use of language and vocabulary and learn to write longer essays. Finally, at the rhetoric stage, older students can learn how to eloquently express themselves in both written and verbal forms.

PROS AND CONS

The advantages of the classical method include the emphasis it puts on the reading and understanding of great books. The classical method is the basis of instruction at liberal arts colleges around the world, which makes it a very generalizable form of education. This method is highly systematic and provides focused content for those who may enjoy a more traditional home learning structure. Many homeschooling families practice the classical method, making it easy to find like-minded individuals within local communities.

The disadvantage of the classical method may be the priority it puts on reading and navigating text. This method may not work well for more unstructured homeschoolers, such as those practicing unschooling. The classical method is rigorous and depends on an elevated level of parental participation and planning. Students with dyslexia or other reading issues may have to access classic books using audio or modified text.

YOU MIGHT LIKE THIS METHOD IF . . .

You might like this method if you are geared toward the educational philosophies of perennialism and essentialism, as it is focused on the teaching of basic skills and the acquisition of ancient forms of knowledge and learning. The classical method can easily be used by faith-based homeschoolers who may appreciate the focus on ancient languages and lessons in moral character. The concentration on classic texts fits well with a multicultural curriculum. Finally, the classical method is the perfect plan for gifted students who enjoy dialogue, debate, and Socratic discussions.

The Charlotte Mason Method

Charlotte Mason (1842-1923) was a British educator and 19th-century homeschooling pioneer. After years of teaching school in England, she became a professor at the Bishop Oxford Training College. There, she gave a series of lectures centering on home education and began to study and write books on the topic. Charlotte Mason was dedicated to providing a Christian-centered, liberal arts education for all students, regardless of social class. She was devoted to equity and access for all.

CORE CONCEPTS

The Charlotte Mason method centers on the whole child, and sees education as "an atmosphere, a discipline, and a life." Mason saw the *atmosphere* as the environment a parent provides for their child, which is one-third of all learning. She believed *discipline* should be focused on the formation of good habits and the consistency of the homeschooling day and week. *Life* referred to living through thoughts and ideas, utilizing books that make subjects come alive.

HOW TO IMPLEMENT THIS MODEL

Students using the Charlotte Mason method read a lot. Through reading, they learn about the use of great language and academic vocabulary. They practice handwriting through writing quotes from great books, including (but not limited to) scripture from the Bible. Students are also exposed to art and music by looking at and analyzing famous works of art and classical music. Learners using the Charlotte Mason method also spend lots of time outdoors, enjoying nature and the gifts it brings. Handicrafts are a part of the Charlotte Mason method, and students may spend time knitting, crocheting, sewing, carving, or inventing their own creations. Although most students spend time doing academic work in the morning and being outdoors in the afternoon, this schedule can be altered according to parent and child preference.

The Charlotte Mason method tends to be teacher-centered and low-tech. Parents will expose their children to great books, music, art, and crafts. They'll also open up discussions about thoughts and ideas coming from those elements. The curriculum can be adapted for students with special needs, who may thrive on the method's focus on consistency, developing habits, and daily schedules. The method tends to be highly systematic, although the schedule of learning can be adapted to suit working parents or others with fixed time commitments.

YOU MIGHT LIKE THIS METHOD IF . . .

You might like this method if you're attracted to a perennialist or essentialist philosophy. Perennialism, or focusing on the teaching and learning of classic ideas, is key to the core curriculum of the Charlotte Mason method. Essentialists may enjoy the focus on teaching and learning core concepts and basic skills, and the traditional and organized structure of the Charlotte Mason method. Faith-based homeschoolers may appreciate the Bible-based focus of the method, and its overall Christian worldview. Gifted and high-achieving students may appreciate the Charlotte Mason method's focus on reading, language, thought, and the use of advanced vocabulary.

The Montessori Method

Maria Montessori (1870-1952) was an Italian physician, feminist, and educator best known for her creation of the Montessori method. Maria Montessori saw education as both manual and intellectual work, and she wanted to create in children a sense of fairness, social justice, and compassion.

This is first done through play and then later on through meaningful cognitive and vocational experiences. It was important to Montessori that students see joy in their everyday work.

CORE CONCEPTS

This method centers on the philosophy that children learn naturally and absorb knowledge from their surroundings. The teacher, child, and environment create a learning triangle, and all are influenced by one another. The teacher provides an environment that supports autonomy, freedom, and order; the child makes use of that environment, using the teacher as a guide.

HOW TO IMPLEMENT THIS MODEL

In the early years of a Montessori education, children will learn through peaceful movement, play, and work with their hands. They will question, think, and learn to take responsibility for their own learning. As they become older, they'll transition to abstract thinking. Adolescent students utilizing the Montessori method will learn about core subjects, as well as immerse themselves in the cultural studies of psychology, anthropology, botany, or zoology. They'll also seek socialization and solidarity with peers, learn to reason and debate, and show an interest in issues of human welfare and dignity.

PROS AND CONS

The Montessori method tends to be student-centered and low-tech. Its focus on play and the creation of a peaceful, calm environment may make it the perfect method for students with disabilities, particularly students with ADHD, autism, or emotional/behavioral disorders. It's a fairly flexible homeschooling method, with parents facilitating rather than being hands-on. The Montessori method is highly effective for parents who naturally maintain a calm, peaceful home environment.

You might like this method if you are attracted to a romanticist teaching philosophy, centering on the ability of students to fulfill their own educational needs. Parents of gifted students may appreciate the focus on core subjects, as well as the cultural studies usually taught only in college. Students of different backgrounds may appreciate the Montessori method for its European influence and feel. Faith-based homeschoolers may value the importance the Montessori method places on human need, social justice, and compassion toward living beings.

Unschooling

John Holt (1923-1985) was an American author and educator. He is also considered the father of the unschooling movement. He coined the term "unschooling" in the 1970s as a play on the popular 7 Up "Uncola" advertisement of that time, when 7 Up was being marketed as something new and different from traditional sodas like Coca-Cola or Pepsi-Cola. So unschooling doesn't mean "no school" just as "uncola" didn't mean no soda; you have school, but it looks very different. Unschooling is a variation of homeschooling. Instead of following a set curriculum, children learn through everyday life experiences. These experiences are of their choosing and tend to match their strengths, interests, and personal learning styles. Unschooling is not "school at home." In unschooling, there are no assignments, no set curricula, and no structured assessments. Within an unschooling environment, parents do not directly teach or provide direct instruction. However, they do provide an environmental context that supports their child's or teen's learning and development.

CORE CONCEPTS

Holt believed that those practicing unschooling should parent respectfully and guide and support learners to control their own lives without punishment or rewards. Unschooling is all about creating an environment where natural learning can flourish. Unschoolers do not establish a curriculum for their children, nor do they require children to do particular assignments or have their children take tests or quizzes as proof of learning. Instead, they allow their children the freedom to pursue their own interests and to learn, in their own way, what they need to know to follow those interests.

HOW TO IMPLEMENT THIS MODEL

How someone unschools really depends on what type of unschooler they define themself to be. Radical unschoolers allow their children to completely create their own day, while relaxed homeschoolers may have their children do some form of structured school-based work. Some unschooling parents have their child create their own schedules for the week ahead so that the parent involved in unschooling can provide an environmental context for the type of learning their child wants to do. For example, if their child wants to study architecture that week, perhaps the child and parent will go to the library at the beginning of the week, borrow lots of books about architecture, and plan field trips to historic houses or churches.

Unschooling is completely student-centered and self-directed. In fact, it is sometimes called self-directed, self-determined, or willed learning. It can be done in a high-tech or low-tech way. Unschooling is beneficial for all students, even students with special needs. However, parents of students with special needs may want to supplement unschooling with particular reading programs, tutoring, or therapy, as needed and wanted. Unschooling is a hands-off form of learning, and is great for the working homeschooling parent who may not have lots of time to devote to lesson planning or grading.

YOU MIGHT LIKE THIS METHOD IF . . .

You might like this method if you're attracted to a romanticist teaching philosophy, which focuses on self-directed learning through real-world experience. Multicultural and multilingual families may appreciate unschooling's dependence on cultural transmission—that is, the passing on of attitudes, beliefs, learning, and language through cultural and familial immersion. Gifted and high-achieving students may enjoy unschooling because it allows the child or teen to pursue their own projects and interests in an in-depth, exploratory way.

The School-at-Home Method

The school-at-home method takes the same approach as public or private school and applies it to homeschooling. For example, within a school-at-home method, a parent serves as a teacher by giving direct instruction to the child or children in their care and will use a curriculum that's similar to or the same as that of their local public or private school. The curricula, assessments, and state-based standards are grade-based and created for groups of same-age individuals on a similar trajectory of social, emotional, and intellectual growth.

CORE CONCEPTS

Because the school-at-home method replicates traditional school structure, parents inherently understand how to schedule a child's day, and the child intrinsically understands and can easily adapt to the daily and weekly schedule. Many school-at-home parents structure the academic day so that school subjects can be completed in the morning, and art, music, physical education, and health education are done in the afternoon.

HOW TO IMPLEMENT THIS MODEL

Implementation is structured and simple. For each subject, the parent homeschooling the child or teen creates daily or weekly lesson plans outlining the specific subject, any materials needed, how it will be taught, and how it will be assessed. The parent then directly instructs the student, using textbook-type materials, worksheets, and direct lectures and discussions. Some students are more self-directed and can teach themselves using the lesson plan and materials provided. The parent then grades and comments on their work.

PROS AND CONS

The school-at-home method can be teacher- or student-centered, depending on how intrinsically motivated the student is to complete their own work. School-at-home can be high- or low-tech, as some parents choose to use textbooks and tactile materials, while other parents depend on a computer-based or formulated curriculum. Some local school districts may even be able to provide curricula or materials to homeschoolers who use this method. As most teacher editions of textbooks contain notes on how to modify the curriculum or make it accessible to children with disabilities, the school-at-home method can be easily adapted for any student. School-at-home tends to be highly systematic and hands-on for both parent and student.

YOU MIGHT LIKE THIS METHOD IF . . .

You might like this method if you're attracted to an essentialist philosophy that focuses on the teaching and learning of core subjects and basic skills. Faith-based homeschoolers sometimes supplement a school-at-home curriculum with religious texts and materials, while multicultural and multilingual homeschoolers may want to choose books and materials that are more culturally relevant and equitable than a traditional school curriculum. High-achieving students may appreciate the school-at-home method for its focus on grades and advanced assessments.

The Unit Studies Method

The unit studies method allows students to learn about one topic at a time in a deep and meaningful way. The unit studies method is unlike both the subject-based learning in school and the school-at-home method. Instead of students learning core subjects in isolation, units of study are introduced as a whole, combining lessons in language, math, science, and history into one specific unit.

CORE CONCEPTS

Within the unit studies method, a topic or element is introduced. Then, the student gets to dive deeply into the topic until they complete the unit. The unit studies method is similar to the method the ancient Greeks used to study thousands of years ago. Studying elements or topics as a whole allows students to grasp the big picture or main idea of a topic and understand how smaller elements work around it.

HOW TO IMPLEMENT THIS MODEL

If the student is studying the sun, for example, they may learn about weather and temperature, but also heat, thermal energy, and the entire solar system. Students may also learn about the different names the sun has had, like Sol, Soleil, and Helios, as well as the linguistic origins of those names. Finally, students will learn about the size of the sun, and be introduced to concepts such as diameter, mass, volume, surface area, and density. Discussions could further include topics like the atmosphere and solar eclipses.

PROS AND CONS

The unit studies method is teacher-centered. The homeschooling parent is primarily responsible for preparing unit plans for the study of a particular topic and for facilitating discussions of that topic. Parents can also buy prepared plans. Unit studies can be done in a low-tech way by using books and tactile materials or in a high-tech way by using online resources. Students with special needs, especially students with high-functioning autism or difficulties with attention, may appreciate focusing on one topic for a particular period. Gifted students may also like the time a unit studies method allows for intensive, concentrated study of a particular subject.

You might like this method if you prefer the philosophy of perennialism, as a unit studies method tends to be a form of classical education; it's a highly discussion-based approach. Faith-based homeschoolers can add religious studies to the unit studies method or can integrate faith-based ideas into the particular unit being studied. Multicultural and multilingual homeschoolers can also add cultural ideas and language study into the study of a topic or element.

The Eclectic Education Method

Although some homeschooling parents pick a specific method that works for them and their child, those who practice the eclectic education method pick and choose from different curricula instead of committing to a specific plan. This allows them the freedom to shape their homeschooling week, and plan their schedule in a way that works for them. It also permits the homeschooling family to make use of elements from different methods, combining them in ways that feel right for their child or children.

CORE CONCEPTS

Eclectic education is truly individualized. This personalized approach takes a child's strengths, learning styles, and interests into full consideration. While some children may thrive in a highly structured system with a methodically planned schedule, others may be at their best with a more loosely structured approach. This is one of the core components of eclectic education: It's all about what works best for each individual.

HOW TO IMPLEMENT THIS MODEL

For example, on Monday, a parent may choose to have a more structured school-at-home-style schedule for their child, while Tuesday through Thursday may involve more unit study–like activities focusing on one topic. Friday may be a more unstructured day, when a child can use an unschooling method to focus on their own individual strengths and interests. The extent and types of structure can also be varied to suit the unique abilities of the child.

PROS AND CONS

Some days, an eclectic method may be more teacher-centered, while other days, learning is more student-centered. Eclectic education can be high- or low-tech, or a combination of both. For example, I know one parent who utilizes a low-tech Charlotte Mason method based on a curriculum of great books on Monday through Thursday but allows her child to unschool on Fridays. Because unschooling is child-led, many Fridays are spent with her child as he builds a model of Mars on the video game Minecraft. An eclectic curriculum can be easily adapted for different students, including those with special needs.

YOU MIGHT LIKE THIS METHOD IF . . .

You might like this method if you want to combine different homeschooling models and different educational philosophies. Learning happens everywhere, in all different ways, and an eclectic method reflects this. Faith-based homeschoolers can add religious studies to any and all methods, and multicultural and multilingual learners can enjoy the freedom the eclectic method gives them to study their heritage and use materials in different languages. Gifted students may also appreciate that the eclectic method allows them to learn and study in a multitude of ways, depending on the day and their particular needs.

How to Pair a Homeschool Model with a Teaching Philosophy

Homeschooling methods are most effective when they line up with the core educational beliefs that guide your educational philosophy. Now that you've learned about different philosophies of education and various homeschooling methods, it's time to pick the combination that works for you! Your answers to the following questions will help guide your choice of method.

» What core educational philosophy do I most align with?

» What method seems like it would be the best for my child or teen and our family?

» Does this method support the educational philosophy I've chosen?

» Can I successfully incorporate the necessary techniques, activities, and types of learning the method requires with the amount of time I can dedicate to homeschooling?

» If we choose a more structured approach, do I have the time to write lesson or unit plans and grade assignments?

» If we choose an unstructured approach, is my child self-directed enough to be in charge of their own learning?

» Should we purchase a curriculum, or do I have the time to organize one on my own?

» If we choose a more eclectic approach, which methods would be complementary to one another and work best for my child?

» What would a typical day look like for us? What would a typical week look like?

» How will I document my child's learning so that I can make sure that each week aligns with the educational philosophy and methods I've chosen?

Homeschooling your child is a big responsibility, but it is also very doable if you're honest about what approach you prefer. It's essential that you choose the method that works for you and your family. Some parents start with a more structured approach and then figure out that a more student-directed, unstructured method works best for them. Other parents start with a student-centered approach, and then realize that their child needs more direct teaching and instruction. Different methods work for different kids and families. Whichever method or combination of methods you decide on, be assured that you're choosing a viable, wonderful alternative to traditional schooling.

Think about how much you've already learned about homeschooling! You've read about the benefits of home learning. You know how important it is to create a learning environment in your own living space. You've crafted your own educational philosophy and researched different methods of home learning.

You're making amazing, educated decisions about your family's homeschooling journey. Bravo to you and the work you are doing now! Next, we'll dive into the topic of state standards and requirements for homeschooling, so you'll know how to meet them when you start homeschooling your child.

CHAPTER FIVE

GENERAL STANDARDS AND REQUIREMENTS

Homeschooling rules and regulations are set by individual states. Although many states standardize curricula, laws are flexible enough so that parents can choose the homeschool model they prefer and create a personalized education plan for their child. For example, when I was homeschooling my son, we lived in New York, which highly regulates home learning. However, we were able to take the curriculum New York required and modify it to fit my son's learning style, interests, and strengths. My son got a quality education, and our local district was always satisfied with our reporting and his test scores. (You'll find helpful guides for navigating state requirements in the resources section of this book—see page 144.)

State Homeschool Laws

Homeschooling has been legal in all 50 states since 1993. Although homeschooling is legal nationwide, each state is in charge of creating its own homeschooling laws. In order to better understand these laws, let's review some terminology you may see within your state's homeschooling regulations.

Compulsory Attendance: Each state has a minimum and maximum age at which a student must be enrolled in and attend school. "School" can mean public school, private school, charter school, or a registered homeschool. For example, in Pennsylvania, compulsory attendance laws are valid from the time a child turns six to the time a child turns 18. In Florida, compulsory attendance laws are valid from 6 to 16 years of age.

Declaration of Intent: In most states, the law requires a parent or guardian who teaches their children at home to submit a Letter of Intent or Declaration of Intent to their State Department of Education or local school district. The state or district generally replies to that letter within a certain amount of time with a copy of state homeschool regulations and a form that homeschooling parents can use to craft their Individualized Home Instruction Plan (IHIP). The IHIP outlines the curriculum a parent will cover in every state-mandated subject during the academic year.

Hours of Instruction: Most states outline specifics regarding the total number of hours of instructional time each week that homeschooling families must provide to their children. If you live in a state that has highly regulated homeschooling laws, hours of instruction have to be documented.

Portfolio: A few states require parents to submit a portfolio of their child or teen's homeschool progress at the end of the academic year. This portfolio contains completed assignments or worksheets, as well as completed assessments that show scholastic progress for each subject. Some families include evidence of extracurricular activities in their child's yearly portfolio.

Scope and Sequence: In order to organize a child's homeschool curriculum for the year, or to fill out an IHIP, some parents create a "scope and sequence" document. *Scope* refers to content to be studied or skills to be mastered within a given year. *Sequence* refers to the order that something is studied. So, for example, a child must understand and master addition, subtraction, multiplication, and division before a parent can move on to teaching a child about order of operations in complex math. Using scope and sequence as a guiding tool makes organizing lesson plans and yearly academic plans easy. Some books also review scope and sequence for each grade level. For example, the author E. D. Hirsch has written *The Core Knowledge Series*, covering preschool to sixth grade, which I highly recommend for those who need scope and sequence ideas.

Standardized Tests: Standardized tests measure the knowledge and skills students are supposed to learn within a specific grade in school. Standardized tests are *norm referenced*, which means your child's score is compared with other students within the same age and grade. Standardized tests can be administered at your local school or at home by a certified teacher or another qualified administrator, based on your state or district's homeschool laws. Usually, the state gives you a few standardized tests you can choose from.

Umbrella Schools: An umbrella school is an educational entity, sometimes a private school, which serves to assist homeschooling families in meeting the requirements of their state's homeschooling regulations. Some umbrella schools provide courses and extracurricular activities to students online or in person, and others can provide families with a high school transcript after successful completion of their program. Umbrella schools vary in cost and offerings.

Now that you know the basic terminology of homeschool rules and regulations, let's discuss other qualifications and requirements of home learning. State-by-state requirements and other helpful information are provided by the Home School Legal Defense Association (HSLDA.org).

Parent Qualifications

One of the biggest myths about homeschooling is that you need a teaching degree to homeschool your child. This is just not true. Managing an entire classroom of 25 to 30 children requires a different skill set than teaching your own child or teen. As a parent, you are fully prepared to homeschool your child, as you know your child's needs best. With regard to regulations, in most states there are no parental requirements to be able to homeschool. However, some states require a few basic educational qualifications, such as having a high school diploma or GED, and/or taking a preparation course in home learning. States with the most stringent parental qualifications include North Dakota, New Mexico, Pennsylvania, Ohio, West Virginia, Virginia, North Carolina, Tennessee, South Carolina, Georgia, and Washington. Washington has the strictest rules regarding parental preparation: A parent must have a high school diploma or GED and possess some college credit, or they must complete a parent qualification course in home education. In addition, a certified teacher must meet with a homeschooled child regularly to assess progress.

Teaching and Subject Requirements

You can choose any method that you would like to homeschool your child. However, most states require that specific core subjects be taught, and many states also have specific regulations regarding additional subjects embedded in the state curriculum. For example, in Vermont the law requires that parents instruct students in English language arts, reading, math, history, science, fine arts, and physical education. But the state also requires instruction in citizenship, United States and Vermont government, health, and American literature. Other states may have foreign language requirements, and fire/bicycle/pedestrian safety requirements.

It's important to remember that although the state outlines the subjects you must teach during the year, how you teach those subjects is up to you and your family, using the homeschool method you've chosen. You can also teach many of these subjects informally and through daily life. For example, fine arts can be studied by attending museums and free concerts. Health can be taught by watching public television specials focused on the human body. History and government can be taught by reading the newspaper. Additionally, most towns and cities have fire safety and bicycle safety days, when emergency service personnel teach citizens fire prevention and rules of the road.

Keeping Education Records

What types of records you keep also depends on state regulations. Highly regulatory states require quarterly reports, or a summary of work done each academic quarter, be sent to and reviewed by the district. These quarterly reports culminate in an end-of-the-year report and summary of progress, as well as the results of any end-of-the-year assessments. Although it seems silly, some states require attendance records, or a record of the days your child has completed academic work. Other states may require you to submit a yearly portfolio, or work samples showing progress that your child has collected into a binder, packet, or electronic folder. The best way to complete educational recording requirements is to not think of them as a chore. Instead, start thinking about them as a journal or daily summary of your child's educational journey, like a baby book that you'd keep of your child's milestones during their first year of life.

Records are handy for more than just district reporting purposes. If your child has special needs and an Individualized Education Plan, academic records are helpful for documenting your child's progress toward individual goals. If your teen plans to go to college, educational records completed during the high school years can assist in your teen's postsecondary journey and help support their college applications.

Assessment and Intervention

Some states have no regulations when it comes to an end-of-the-year assessment. Other states may ask for a written summary of progress made or an end-of-the-year portfolio. More highly regulated states will require standardized test scores for specific grades at the end of the year, with your choice of which test to give. In New York, for example, homeschooling families can choose from the Iowa Test of Basic Skills, the California Achievement Test, the Comprehensive Test of Basic Skills, the Metropolitan Achievement Test, or the Personalized Achievement Summary System (PASS) test. When

I homeschooled my son, I always chose the PASS test, as it was simple to administer, and scoring was fast and efficient.

If a child or teen is not showing progress based on the results of an assessment, most states allow for retesting or portfolio/summary resubmission. If, after resubmission, the state or board of education still feels your child is not making progress, they may put you on "probation" for a period until adequate progress is being made. If a homeschooling family gets put on probation, the district will send a letter giving the family a specific period for their child to make adequate academic progress. Some states include home visits from a district representative as part of a probationary period. If adequate progress is not made, some states can refuse the right to allow you to homeschool, under the grounds of "educational neglect." However, in the vast majority of cases, all goes well and the district accepts the results of assessment with no questions asked.

Remember, assessment itself is never something you should fear. Instead, assessment serves as an indicator of your child's strengths and specific needs. Assessment also allows you to ask yourself:

» Are we meeting our goals for home learning?

» Does the curriculum or homeschool method we are using fit our needs?

» How was the year overall? Did my child seem to learn and grow a lot? Or are there any specific needs we need to address in the next school year?

Every good homeschooling family will do some reflection on the year in order to celebrate successes and plan for the next homeschool year ahead!

CHAPTER SIX

SET AND TRACK YOUR HOMESCHOOL GOALS

Goals are important for measuring successes and learning from failures. Goals serve as guides, allowing us to look at things we want our child to learn, and to monitor progress as we go. For example, when my son was in the early elementary grades, it was important for me that he really know basic math facts, including multiplication up to 12 times 12. We practiced an unschooling model, so I didn't use lots of worksheets to get to our goal. Instead, I created a copy of the times table chart found in most composition books and showed my son how to utilize it. We sang multiplication songs and played multiplication games. I encouraged him to use multiplication within the real world at the grocery store and while measuring ingredients for baking. If something cost $2, and I wanted to buy four of them, I would have him do the math. Did he get answers correct every time? Nope! Part of learning is making mistakes. But with consistent practice, he got there. By the end of his third-grade year, my son knew his times tables up to 12 times 12, a skill that has traveled with him through adulthood.

SMART Homeschool Goals

One way to create meaningful goals for your child is to think of the acronym SMART.

SMART stands for:

Specific: Stating exactly what you want your child to accomplish

Measurable: Creating clear goals with easy progress tracking

Attainable: Making sure your goal is realistic for your child or teen

Relevant: Having your goal align with your overall mission or objective

Time-Bound: Creating a deadline for completion of the goal

You can create yearly, quarterly, monthly, weekly, or daily goals for your child and track them using the SMART strategy.

One of the ways you can break down the SMART strategy is by writing out your goal in paragraph form. Then, make sure that all elements of SMART are within your paragraph, and label those elements. Here's an example of a quarterly goal written out in SMART strategy:

EXAMPLE Quarterly SMART Homeschool Goal

This year in math, I want my fourth-grade daughter to learn dividing with remainders (Specific). She already knows addition, subtraction, multiplication, and her basic division facts, and is ready for dividing with remainders (Attainable). We already have a progress tracking system: At the end of each week I give her 10 math problems to complete as an informal assessment, and we calculate the number correct and put it in an Excel spreadsheet. If she gets an 9/10 or better, we go out for a treat Friday afternoon, either at a local coffee shop or ice cream place (Measurable). We utilize a school-at-home method, and I think it's important to stick to grade-based standards when it comes to specific subjects (Relevant). We will have this goal completed at the end of our first quarter of fourth grade, in the last week of October (Time-Bound).

The most efficient way to learn to write SMART goals is with frequent and consistent practice. Over time, writing and applying SMART goals becomes more intuitive and creates a useful framework for outlining short-term and long-term educational goals. We'll review a couple of goals within this chapter.

Here's an example of a weekly goal broken down using the SMART Strategy:

EXAMPLE Weekly SMART Homeschool Goal

Goal for the week: Improve Kayla's multistep word problem skills

SMART breakdown:

Specific: By Friday, Kayla will accurately solve multistep word problems

Measurable: At the end of two lessons, Kayla will be able to identify essential information within word problems. At the end of three lessons, Kayla will correctly identify the operations needed to solve the word problem. At the end of five lessons, Kayla will have the skills to accurately solve at least $8/10$ multistep word problems.

Achievable: Kayla can already solve one-step word problems with 100 percent accuracy, so it's time to move to multistep word problems.

Relevant: We use the classical method to homeschool and follow sequenced instruction within that curriculum. Also, Kayla will have to solve word problems many times throughout her academic career.

Time-Bound: We'll practice this skill all week and assess at the end of the week.

Restating, in paragraph form:

> *Our goal this week is to improve Kayla's completion of multistep word problem skills. We want her to accurately solve multistep word problems by the end of the week* **(Specific)**. *At the end of two lessons, Kayla will be able to identify essential information within word problems. At the end of three lessons, Kayla will correctly identify the operations needed to solve the word problem. At the end of five lessons, Kayla will have the skills to accurately solve at least 8 of 10 multistep word problems. We want Kayla to*

feel intrinsically proud of her progress, but we'll also provide praise for her good work **(Measurable)**. *Kayla can already solve one-step word problems with 100 percent accuracy, so it's time to move to multistep word problems* **(Achievable)**. *We use the classical method to homeschool and follow sequenced instruction within that curriculum. Learning how to solve multistep word problems is the next step according to the math textbook we are using* **(Relevant)**. *Together, we'll practice this skill for a half hour a day and assess the skill at the end of the week* **(Time-Bound)**.

Here is another SMART homeschool goal example, in daily form:

EXAMPLE *Daily SMART Homeschool Goal*

Goal for today: Work on Jay's reading comprehension skills

SMART breakdown:

Specific: By the end of the day, Jay will be able to determine the main idea of the book *My Side of the Mountain* by Jean Craighead George.

Measurable: After reading five chapters of *My Side of the Mountain*, Jay will be able to verbally express the main idea of the book with 100 percent accuracy.

Achievable: Last month, Jay was able to correctly identify and discuss the main idea of *The Horse and His Boy* by C. S. Lewis, so he should be able to identify the main idea of *My Side of the Mountain*, even though the ideas within this book are a bit more advanced.

Relevant: We use the Charlotte Mason method to homeschool and rely on a curriculum of great books. *My Side of the Mountain* was identified as a "next step" book for Jay and is considered a classic.

Time-Bound: Our work today centers on *My Side of the Mountain*, so we'll spend a good part of the day reading and discussing the book.

Restating, in paragraph form:

> *Our goal today is to have Jay determine the main idea of Jean Craighead George's book* My Side of the Mountain ***(Specific)***. *He plans to read five chapters today, and after reading those chapters, the expectation is that Jay will be able to verbally express the main idea of the book with 100 percent accuracy* ***(Measurable)***. *Last month, Jay was able to correctly identify and discuss the main idea of* The Horse and His Boy *by C. S. Lewis, so he should be able to identify the main idea of* My Side of the Mountain, *even though the ideas within this book are a bit more advanced* ***(Achievable)***. *We use the Charlotte Mason method to homeschool and rely on a curriculum of great books.* My Side of the Mountain *was identified as a "next step" book for Jay, and is considered a classic* ***(Relevant)***. *Our work today will focus on the book and we'll spend a good part of the day reading and discussing this work* ***(Time-Bound)***.

Practical Ways to Track Success

Progress tracking is an important part of measuring goal attainment. In fact, studies show that when student achievement is displayed graphically, there's a 26-point gain in achievement over time. Moreover, when students get involved in tracking their own progress, there's a 32-point gain in achievement over time. That's a lot of points gained!

Tracking progress is fun and easy for both parents and students!

Let's go back to our first quarterly SMART homeschool goal example, in which a fourth grader is learning how to divide with remainders.

First, it will be up to the parent to break down the goal into small steps, reviewing basic division facts and progressing to dividing with remainders. Then, the parent will monitor daily progress. For example, if the parent gives a student five division questions each day, they'll count how many answers the child gets correct. At first, the fourth grader may only get one or two correct answers, but eventually that number will increase as practice makes perfect!

Daily progress monitoring done each day will turn into weekly progress monitoring. If a parent is following a traditional school-at-home method, Friday may be the day when a parent gives the student a 10-question quiz, making weekly progress monitoring easy.

In our example, the parent has decided that Friday is also "treat" day, so if the student gets an 8/10 or better, she gets to go to the coffee shop or ice cream parlor and pick out an item she likes as a reward. Extrinsic rewards are really motivating for some students!

And, of course, once students achieve a goal, it's time to move forward to another goal! That is a reward in and of itself.

How to Pair a Homeschool Model with Educational Goals

It's important to note that SMART goal tracking isn't going to work for everyone. However, if you're utilizing a more formal, teacher-led homeschooling model, like the school-at-home method, the Charlotte Mason method, classical homeschooling, or the unit studies method, goal tracking may be helpful. In addition, although progress monitoring and external reward systems are helpful for some students, other students will be more intrinsically motivated and will want to monitor their own goals in a way that works for them.

Therefore, ask yourself these important questions before you pair a homeschool model with educational goals:

» What model works best when considering our personal family values?

» What educational philosophy am I most comfortable with? What would work best for my child?

» Do I plan to homeschool for one year, or could I see myself continuing to homeschool my child if this is working for us?

» What does our home and family situation look like? What model would work the best for our family?

» How much flexibility do I want as a parent? Would I prefer to create daily lesson plans that my child has to follow, or would I prefer a model that is more student-directed?

» What motivational system would be best for my child? Does my child work better with extrinsic rewards, or is my child more intrinsically motivated?

Finally, look back at the educational philosophy statement you wrote in chapter 3, combine it with the homeschool model you have chosen, and think about the following questions:

» How does this homeschool model support my teaching or educational philosophy?

» How will the model I chose support my child's strengths?

» How will the model address any learning or academic needs my child has?

» Will my child or teen enjoy the model chosen?

If you've chosen a homeschool model that supports your child's strengths and needs, and it matches well with your personal educational philosophy, bravo! You're ready to dive into the incredible world of home learning. If you need to rethink your philosophy or reconsider the model you've chosen, don't worry at all! Look at the models again, and compare them with your philosophy. Most important, call in your child or teen and review the models with them. What looks interesting to them? Which models are they interested in exploring more? Sometimes, our kids know the answers better than we do.

CHAPTER SEVEN

CREATE YOUR HOMESCHOOL ACTION PLAN

Action plans are valuable blueprints that can guide you on your path to success. I personally love to-do lists, and you can think of a homeschool action plan as an expanded homeschooling to-do list. (If you're someone who doesn't love the idea of creating lists, don't worry. I'm going to help you through this!) I kept three copies of my action plan in different places so I could reference it frequently. The first copy went into my daily planner or calendar. The second copy I posted above our home-school workspace, and the third copy went into a file folder where I kept all the homeschooling paperwork for our district.

Almost 10 years later, I still have a copy of each yearly action plan I created, and I'm glad I saved them all. The action plan truly assisted in my son's journey to college. It was helpful not only to review our homeschooling goals each year, but also to see what I was thinking during each year we homeschooled. My son, who is now 24, keeps his own form of an action plan for himself as he navigates writing a thesis for graduate school. He also uses an action plan for each of the students in the music school he runs. His homeschooling years provided him with an action plan model that he could modify and take with him to adulthood. This chapter will give you the tools to create an action plan for your learner.

What Is a Homeschool Action Plan?

A homeschool action plan is a proposed strategy or course of action that helps you, as a homeschooling parent, set, track, and develop goals for your child. While I was a homeschooling parent, I always created two different action plans. One contained my responsibilities and plan for school district reporting for the year, and the other was a subject-based homeschooling action plan that outlined content and goals for our homeschool year. If you live in a state with little to no homeschooling regulations, you may not need the Action Plan for District or State Reporting. But if you live in a state that is moderately to highly regulatory, the Action Plan for District or State Reporting will keep you on track.

The Action Plan for District or State Reporting contains the following items:

» Mission statement

» Homeschool method

» Letter of intent to homeschool

» Quarterly reporting dates

» End-of-the-year summary

» Final assessment due date

» Reflection

The Subject-Based Homeschooling Action Plan contains the following items:

» Subject

» Goal description or summary of yearly goals

» Resources to use

» Specific learning needs or material-based needs

» Objectives or tasks to achieve the goal

» Plan for progress monitoring (daily, weekly, monthly, or quarterly)

» Criteria for success

» Deadline for meeting goals

» Reflection

Create a Mission Statement

You'll want to begin your action plan with a homeschool mission statement. A homeschool mission statement is a paragraph stating what you plan to accomplish, and why, within your home learning environment. You can use your educational philosophy as a start, and identify what you believe about learning and education. Then you can reflect on why you chose the homeschool model you did. You can end with what you hope to accomplish this school year with your child, including short-term and longer-term goals.

Below is an example of a homeschool mission statement:

I am a romanticist and believe that learning should happen in a real-life context. I want my child to follow his own intrinsic interests, which is why we choose unschooling as our homeschooling model. However, I also want to bring in ideas from other philosophies, which makes us eclectic, as well. I like the Montessori focus on the interaction between people and the environment, and I appreciate the reading of great books as outlined within the Charlotte Mason method. This year, it's my hope that my teen will enjoy some classic books and start to learn a second language, based on his interest in learning Japanese. He's excited to learn about more advanced math topics through Khan Academy on his own, and I'll be there to help support him. He'll learn history from daily reading and discussion of The New York Times *and any books he shows an interest in. I like the idea of "living history" and will plan field trips so he can experience time in another era. He is taking some astronomy classes through an online learning platform and has expressed interest in exploring biology coursework, too. I feel like my role as a parent is to support his interests and strengths. I'm excited to observe all he learns this year and I will document everything using this action plan and a journal.*

How to Write an Effective Homeschool Action Plan

Now that you've crafted a mission statement using the example above for inspiration, let's tackle your two action plans. The Action Plan for District or State Reporting is easy. It basically comes from state regulations and the information your district gives you once you send in your letter of intent to homeschool (see chapter 5). Some districts will set their own dates for quarterly reporting, and others will allow *you* to set the dates. If you are working on a nine-month homeschool year starting in September, quarterly reporting dates are usually around November 1, January 1, April 1, and June 15. The annual assessment and/or end-of-the-year summary is also due around June 15.

Within your Action Plan for District or State Reporting, it's also important you choose the type of assessment you plan to give your child, based on options your state or district gives. Try to ask other homeschooling parents about their experiences with the different assessments before you decide on one for your own child. Finally, provide space on your Action Plan for District or State Reporting for reflection. At the end of the year, did all go as planned? Did the reporting dates and end-of-the-year assessment you chose work for you and your child? What might make you or your child better prepared next year?

The Subject-Based Homeschooling Action Plan is more in-depth and contains yearly goals for each specific subject area. You'll list yearly goals for each subject, as well as the resources you plan to use. You will also list specific learning needs or material-based needs for each subject area, as well as the tasks you plan to use to get your child to their goal. Then you can form a plan for progress monitoring and list the criteria for success. You'll set a deadline for the goal to be met, as well as a space for reflection at the end of the year.

With these examples, you're equipped to create an action plan for homeschooling! In the next chapter, we'll explore how to shape your plan for your individual learner.

EXAMPLES *Homeschool Action Plan*

Below you will find two completed action plans. One is a completed Action Plan for State or District Homeschool Reporting, and the other is a Subject-Based Homeschooling Action Plan based on our mission statement example. I hope you'll find these examples helpful in your own planning!

ACTION PLAN FOR STATE OR DISTRICT HOMESCHOOL REPORTING

Homeschool Mission Statement

I am a romanticist and believe that learning should happen in a real-life context. I want my child to follow his own intrinsic interests, which is why we choose unschooling as our homeschooling model. However, I also want to bring in ideas from other philosophies, which makes us eclectic, as well. I like the Montessori focus on the interaction between people and the environment, and I appreciate the reading of great books as outlined within the Charlotte Mason method. This year, it's my hope that my teen will enjoy some classic books and start to learn a second language, based on his interest in learning Japanese. He's excited to learn about more advanced math topics through Khan Academy on his own, and I'll be there to help support him. He'll learn history from daily reading and discussion of The New York Times *and any books he shows an interest in. I like the idea of "living history" and will plan field trips so he can experience time in another era. He is taking some astronomy classes through an online learning platform and has expressed interest in exploring biology coursework, too. I feel like my role as a parent is to support his interests and strengths. I'm excited to observe all he learns this year and I will document everything using this action plan and a journal.*

Date: *July 1*

1st Quarter: *November 1*

2nd Quarter: *January 1*

3rd Quarter: *April 1*

4th Quarter: *June 15*

Due: *June 15*

Type of Summary: *Written summary of coursework*

Due: *June 15*

Type of Assessment: *PASS Test*

To be completed after June 15

SUBJECT-BASED HOMESCHOOLING ACTION PLAN

SUBJECT	GOAL	RESOURCES	LEARNING NEEDS
English Language Arts	Completion of 9th grade language arts coursework	9th grade reading list books	Sometimes audiobooks are preferred
History	Completion of 9th grade history coursework	United States history and geography textbook The New York Times	Prefers living history, planning of field trips needed
Science	Completion of 9th grade science coursework	Astronomy Outschool Course Biology textbook	Preference for interactive science work on the computer

TASKS TO GOAL	PLAN FOR PROGRESS MONITORING	CRITERIA FOR SUCCESS	REFLECTION
Reading of 3 books per quarter Daily vocab review Daily writing exercise	Quarterly progress monitoring discussion with student Weekly discussion of books read	Successful completion of coursework with 80% accuracy	It helps if I read the required books with him so we can have an educated discussion.
Reading of 5 chapters per quarter Planning of 3 American History–based field trips	Discussion of each chapter Verbal and written comprehension tasks each week	Successful completion of coursework and field trips	We just did our first field trip to the battlefield. It was a success!
Completion of online astronomy course Reading of 5 chapters per quarter Living Brain Exhibit at local history museum	Astronomy: self-monitored discussion of each chapter Biology: completion of quiz at the end of the chapter	Successful completion of Outschool course, coursework, and field trips	Ben loves when science comes alive. Plan more field trips!

CONTINUED >>

SUBJECT	GOAL	RESOURCES	LEARNING NEEDS
Math	Completion of 9th grade math coursework	Algebra for All Resources Khan Academy Video	Preference for Khan Academy and computer-based math
Health Education	Completion of 9th grade health coursework	Online resources plus family discussions	Prefers rooting conversation in current articles
Foreign Language (Japanese)	Completion of foreign language requirement	Rosetta Stone and Duolingo	Preference for digital language learning, practicing on phone
Fine Arts	Completion of fine arts requirement	Field trips to museums plus music lessons	Preference for interactive work

TASKS TO GOAL	PLAN FOR PROGRESS MONITORING	CRITERIA FOR SUCCESS	REFLECTION
Complete algebra coursework on Khan Academy, including study of angles, area, order of operations, means, and standard deviation Use 5 Algebra for All modules	Khan Academy and Algebra for All quizzes weekly	Successful completion of Khan Academy and Algebra for All coursework with at least 80% accuracy	I would like to add some math for everyday life into our curriculum.
Complete coursework on alcohol, tobacco, and drug misuse, as well as sexuality and acceptance Complete coursework on bullying	Constant discussion, self-monitoring	Successful completion of health topic requirement	I'd also like to include conversations about nutrition and living a healthy life.
Completion of Rosetta Stone Part 1 and continued practice on Duolingo	Self-monitoring, conversations with friend from Japan	Successful completion of 16 levels on Duolingo (a self-created criterion)	Ben wants to learn more about Japanese culture, as well as language.
Completion of half of the guitar scales book he is working on	Self-monitoring	Successful completion of half of the guitar scales book; trips to at least 2 art museums	There is so much art within our community. We both would like to explore that more.

CHAPTER EIGHT

PERSONALIZE AN ACTION PLAN FOR YOUR CHILD'S NEEDS

The curricula and state-based standards found in schools are created for groups of same-age students on a similar trajectory of social, emotional, and intellectual growth. For example, a seventh-grade curriculum is created for the "average" 12-year-old, without taking into consideration individual interests, strengths, needs, and talents. Parents often pick homeschooling as an alternative because they want to personalize education for their own unique child. In fact, the most wonderful thing about home learning is that it allows parents to give their children an education that matches their individual learning styles.

I chose homeschooling for my son because I wanted to give him an education that made sense for him: an education full of books, interesting people, and life experiences. Although everyone thought I was choosing homeschooling to shelter my son from life, I knew I was choosing homeschooling to expose him to life in the real world.

Homeschooling also allowed my son the time and space to dive deeply into his interests. Through his love of rocks, he learned chemistry. Through his love of coins and money, he learned about math and historical figures. Through his love of golf, he learned about yardage, landscape, and topography. Everything was a learning experience. What an amazing gift, to be able to look at life that way! That is the gift you will be giving your child when you choose to homeschool.

In each of the following explorations, you'll find a "best practices" section. Best practices are what they sound like: ideas that have been proven effective or helpful.

Faith-Based Homeschool Plans

In previous years, being able to provide a faith-based education was one of the primary reasons parents decided to homeschool their children. In fact, when most people thought of homeschooling in the late 1990s and early 2000s, they mostly associated it with devout Christians. In 2021, instilling religious values is still one of the top reasons parents choose to homeschool their child or teen. However, the population of faith-based homeschoolers has become more diverse as homeschooling has increased in popularity.

You can adapt any homeschool model to incorporate a focus on faith. For example, I know many Catholic unschoolers who explore stories and artwork incorporating saints during the school days and integrate morning and evening prayer into their routines. I also know many Muslim families who choose to homeschool instead of sending their children to private Islamic schools. One of my best homeschooling friends integrated the learning of Hebrew and the tenets of Judaism into her children's days. There are many faith-based homeschoolers who maintain blogs or YouTube channels to document their home learning activities. You may want to find a few that homeschool in a similar style using a faith basis.

Ideas to Think About

- » *How will this plan support my definition of education?* Faith is such an important part of many people's lives. How will integrating faith into your homeschool model align with the definition of education you created when writing your educational philosophy statement?

- » *How will this plan help me address important educational challenges?* Prayer or meditation is an essential part of most belief systems and can assist in coping with the realities of life. How will you integrate prayer and meditation into the homeschooling day?

- » *Will faith-based homeschooling help accomplish my homeschooling goals?* Imagine a day using the homeschool model you've chosen and integrating faith into that model. How will this help accomplish the specific homeschooling goals for you and your child? Is the model you chose complementary to your faith-based lifestyle?

Best Practices

» Integrate prayer or meditation into your child's everyday life. Remember, children learn by observation. The more you make prayer or meditation a daily practice, the higher chance that they will, too.

» Use your holy texts in different ways. Holy texts are not just for reading. You can assist your child in memorizing verses. Or you can have them use holy texts for copy work, for handwriting practice and to learn about sentence structure and grammar through "copying" a model. Have older students make connections from holy texts to more secular books they may have read.

» Ultimately, all faiths are about social justice and acts of kindness and peace. Create opportunities for your child or teen to volunteer at their church, mosque, or synagogue, or within the community. Volunteering is a wonderful way to help others and learn new skills.

» Allow your child to explore different faiths and cultures, especially in the teen years. During this exploration, they can find, compare, and discuss similarities and differences between their faith and the beliefs of others, allowing them to expand their worldview.

» MuslimHomeschoolersUnite.com is a wonderful site for those integrating the word of Allah into their home-schooling lives. I especially love the website's Muslim Morning Time Menus, a choice-based approach to Muslim homeschooling for all ages.

» Sonlight.com is one of the most popular curriculum companies for Christian homeschoolers. Its curriculum for pre-K through grade 12 is based on the Bible and rich with many fantastic resources.

» CatholicSchoolhouse.com provides Catholic-based supplemental learning activities and resources for those using classical or school-at-home models. The website offers free webinars and a virtual community for Catholic homeschoolers to share tips and gain support.

» JewishEducationatHome on YouTube is an incredible channel of homeschooling videos geared especially for Jewish parents. The channel includes a homeschooling house tour, a discussion of Jewish beliefs and practices, and an introduction to different home learning models.

» The National Home Education Resource Institute (NHERI.org) is a nonprofit Christian research orga-nization run by Dr. Brian Ray. NHERI specializes in homeschool research, facts, statistics, and information. It is a wonderful resource for those seeking academic data on home learning.

» GlobalVillageSchool.org provides Buddhist and Univer-salist home learners with a distance learning curriculum and diploma-based home learning program. The Global

Village School curriculum integrates themes such as self-knowledge, social justice, and sustainability into core subjects.

Multicultural and Multilingual Homeschool Plans

Homeschooled students come from many cultures and some are fluent in more than one language. More and more people are choosing homeschooling to immerse their children in their native culture and language. In fact, homeschooling has always been rooted in an appreciation of the benefits of cultural transmission. Cultural transmission occurs without formal teaching; it is a way of learning and passing on information through family or cultural norms. Language learning also occurs through cultural transmission. Multilingual homeschooling allows children and teens the opportunity to become bilingual, which will be a great benefit to these students in their later lives and future careers.

Ideas to Think About

» *How will multicultural and multilingual homeschooling support my definition of education?* Go back to your educational philosophy statement. Was multicultural education or appreciation of culture and language included? Education is all about enhancing one's mind and perspective, and having a multicultural/multilingual education assists in this.

» *How will this plan help me address important educational challenges?* Will your child appreciate the learning of another language within a system of multicultural education? Or will additional language learning be challenging for them? Sometimes, students with dyslexia or other learning disabilities have a hard time learning a second language when they're still mastering a first language. This is something to consider, but it shouldn't stop you from practicing multilingual and multicultural homeschooling if it's important to you and your family.

» *Will multilingual/multicultural homeschooling help accomplish my homeschooling goals?* Many colleges, universities, and workplaces see multicultural and multilingual education as an asset to a college application or résumé. Will this form of home learning assist you and your child in accomplishing your homeschooling goals? Is it complementary to the homeschooling model or method you've chosen?

Best Practices

» Give your child or teen opportunities outside the family unit to practice language skills or deepen cultural ties. Cultural festivals, parades, and cultural centers are amazing places for your child to use their skills and knowledge.

» Go to museums and check out art and artifacts from different cultures, or log on to a museum's website and do a virtual tour! Discuss the use and purpose of these artifacts within the daily life of a specific cultural group.

» Traveling is an amazing way to explore other cultures and languages. There is a wonderful "worldschooling" community within the homeschooling community that embraces those who would like to live a travel-based, multicultural, and multilingual lifestyle.

» Cook with your children and give them access to family recipes that span generations. I lived in a multilingual household when I was younger, and although I couldn't speak my grandmother's language, I could watch her cook. I still cook many of the same meals she would make for me when I was a child.

RESOURCES

» Project World School (ProjectWorldSchool.com), the brainchild of worldschooler Laine Liberti and her son Miro Siegal, is a two- to four-week retreat program that is open to adolescents and young adults ages 13 to 25. The mission of Project World School is to provide international learning experiences for adolescents and young adults with a strong emphasis on cooperative learning, co-creation, community, and social learning. The retreats focus on offering a deeper cultural immersion that differs from a regular tourist experience. Homeschooled teens perform volunteer and community service work while traveling.

» Akilah Richard's book *Raising Free People: Unschooling as Liberation and Healing Work* discusses the need to build new structures and systems of education. It examines issues such as the decolonization of education, blackness, and cultural community building. Akilah also keeps a blog at RaisingFreePeople.com.

» MommyMaestra.com is an essential resource for those homeschoolers interested in educating their child in English and Spanish. The blog focuses on the experiences of bilingual home learning. It also contains reviews of English and Spanish curriculum choices and children's books.

» Bilingual-Babies.com is a blog dedicated to bilingual and trilingual education and parenting. It's written by a mom who has a PhD in linguistics. You'll find information on bilingual living and homeschooling, as well as specific resources for those interested in the German language.

» Duolingo is a language learning app that's phone- and iPad-friendly, visually accessible, and lots of fun. A student can choose to learn one of many languages Duolingo offers. You'll find a focus on vocabulary and sentence structure, and there are assessments at the end of each lesson. This is gamification of language learning at its best.

» One of my favorite TED talks is Mia Nacamulli's "The Benefits of a Bilingual Brain." This short speech discusses the neurobiology of language learning and the advantages of learning second and third languages.

Homeschool Plans for Special Needs

Homeschooling can offer special needs students flexibility and attention. Also, the home learning environment is personalized and creates an individualized forum to address strengths, interests, and needs. More parents of children with special needs are choosing homeschooling than ever before, seeing the home environment as a place of healing and learning. In 2015, approximately 12 percent of the population of homeschoolers chose homeschooling because of their children's special needs, including physical or mental health needs, and that number is growing every day.

Ideas to Think About

» *How will the home learning environment support my teaching of a child with special needs and help me address important educational challenges?* Homeschooling parents do not need to go at it alone. Many school districts will assist with supplemental services and support. To receive these services, your child must be registered in your school district. So if your child needs a special reading program, your district can help. Your district may also provide speech, counseling, and physical and occupational therapy services. If you don't know whether your child is eligible to receive services, know that under federal law, local school districts are required to provide free evaluation services to students who are homeschooled.

» *Which teaching philosophy or model should I follow when homeschooling a child with disabilities?* In chapters 3 and 4, we reviewed homeschooling philosophies and models, noting that most can be adapted for your child's specific needs. The right model or philosophy is the one that works best for you and your child. Homeschooling a child with disabilities has so many benefits. As long as your child's individual needs are being met through the learning environment you provide and the supports your district or community provides for you, you are in good shape!

» *How will homeschooling my child with special needs help you accomplish my educational goals?* If you're considering homeschooling your child with special needs, most likely the schooling provided to them now is not allowing them to thrive. Every parent wants to see their child succeed. The traditional school environment is sometimes not the best fit or least restrictive environment for some children, but home might be. Homeschooling also allows for increased flexibility in presenting a curriculum in ways that make the most sense for you and your child. This can result in a more efficient, joyful, and mutually beneficial educational journey.

Best Practices

» Before considering home learning, read more about your child's specific disability. What challenges do they face? What strengths do they have? How can your child's strengths and interests assist in addressing the disability? For example, one mom I know has a child with ADHD. The child loved to run and play basketball. Every morning before working on specific subjects, the mom and her son would shoot hoops or run around the block together for half an hour. Then, he would be better focused and able to do his work.

» Most special education teachers spend most of their coursework in undergraduate and graduate school learning how to modify instruction to meet their students' needs. Learn the basics of differentiation—that is, how to tailor instruction to different student needs. Create ways for your child to access whatever curriculum you choose fully and in an enjoyable way.

» Seek support! You can choose from the many support groups in your community and online that focus on homeschooling a child with special needs. Join one, or a few, and connect with like-minded parents who are doing the same thing you are.

RESOURCES

» Understood.org is dedicated to providing information and support for parents and teachers of students with special needs. There are also several articles and videos on the website focused specifically on homeschooling children with learning differences.

» Students with dyslexia and their parents may enjoy the Yale Center for Dyslexia and Creativity (Dyslexia.Yale. edu). This website provides resources, research, and success stories about dyslexia, as well as resources specific to home learning with a dyslexic child.

» Bookshare.org provides free books in braille and audiobooks for children in the United States with a visual impairment or other qualifying disability. Their e-book and audiobook collection is vast, and many home learners enjoy Bookshare's selection of titles and accessibility options.

» SPEDHomeschool.com provides resources and support for parents and students who are home learning, including Individualized Education Plan guides and templates, a homeschooling podcast, and an online homeschooling community.

» Time4Learning.com/homeschooling/special-needs offers specialized curriculum choices for homeschoolers, including text-to-speech options and on-board writing tools. It's also a certified homeschool resource for students with autism.

» HSLDA.org/teaching-my-kids/special-needs offers special tips for homeschooling students, including articles on planning, evaluating, and recordkeeping with Individualized Education Plans. Educational consultants are also available to provide one-on-one guidance and access to inventories, transcript services, and accommodation support.

Homeschool Plans for Gifted and High-Achieving Students

Gifted and high-achieving students can frustrate teachers by underperforming because classes are too easy for them. They also tend to want to go more deeply into a topic or subject than a school period may allow. Gifted students have unique needs that are well served by an individualized homeschool plan.

Ideas to Think About

» *How will home learning support your definition of education?* Education is about more than just learning curriculum. Gifted students tend to want to dive deeply into topics, exploring and understanding all angles of them. They also crave conversation and critical thinking. Review the educational philosophy statement you wrote with your child or teen. What do they agree with? What do they need more of?

» *How will homeschooling assist in addressing important educational challenges?* Gifted students tend to spend lots of time in their heads thinking, absorbing, and understanding. However, they also may need social and emotional support, and some sort of physical outlet. How will you integrate these elements into your home-schooling day?

» *How will this plan help accomplish your educational goals?* Many families choose home learning for their gifted children because the children crave more intellectual stimulation than they are currently getting in school. What does your child need to succeed in a home learning environment? Is it a more project-based learning curriculum? Is it more conversation about specific topics? Is it more real-world or volunteer learning activities? Integrate what your child needs to help them accomplish their educational goals.

Best Practices

» Allow your child to have some choice in what they study, as well as how they study. Have your child review homeschool models with you. Which model may best fit their academic needs?

» Integrate art, music, and theater into lessons. Cross-curricular studies are especially important for gifted students so that they can make cultural connections to what they're learning. Make live or virtual visits to museums a common occurrence, attend live or virtual concerts, and watch live or televised theater performances.

» Find informative online resources and use them as a part of your homeschool practice. Online resources often add multisensory components, something that can be especially important for gifted and high-achieving students. When selecting these resources, consider the learning styles that work best for your child. For instance, are they more visually oriented? Do they prefer text, audio, or video? Make note of your child's preferred learning styles and use them as a guide when selecting resources.

» Look into part-time enrollment in a community college or university for students in grades 11 and up. Enrolling in a community college course or online college course is a wonderful way for your gifted child to explore their interests in a structured environment. Plus, they can get a head start on earning college credits.

» Don't forget social and emotional needs and the need for physical exercise! It's easy for gifted students to be trapped in their own thoughts for extended periods. Make sure your child or teen has a social-emotional outlet, as well as a physical outlet, even if it's just time walking, hiking, or biking outside.

RESOURCES

» When I think of homeschooling gifted students, especially twice-exceptional students (gifted students with disabilities), I often think of Jade Rivera, an author, educator, and coach who designs innovative learning environments for gifted students. Her blog has so many wonderful ideas about educating gifted students, especially those interested in science, technology, engineering, and mathematics (STEM) fields. Her website is JadeAnnRivera.com.

» Cindy West's book *Homeschooling Gifted Kids: A Practical Guide to Educate and Motivate Advanced Learners* is an incredible resource. In her book, she discusses providing challenging curricula, offering social-emotional outlets, and choosing early college classes for gifted students. She also discusses the nurturing of artistic and creative talents in gifted kids.

» Colleen Kessler's podcast *Raising Lifelong Learners* (RaisingLifelongLearners.com) is one of my favorites! Colleen is a homeschooling parent of gifted children, and she has such amazing insights. My favorite of her podcasts center on managing perfectionism in gifted kids, creating homeschool transcripts, and nurturing resiliency.

» Hoagies' Gifted Education Page (HoagiesGifted.org) is a quirky but fantastic resource for all things related to homeschooling gifted children. It contains many articles, ideas, and resources for those interested in home learning and gifted education.

» Mira Alameddine's TED talk, "On Our Gifted Children," discusses the many needs gifted students have, including the needs for academic enrichment and social-emotional coping skills. She calls for a more tolerant, self-directed learning space for gifted students, which home learning can provide.

CHAPTER NINE

YOUR HOMESCHOOL'S NUTS AND BOLTS

Figuring out a homeschool curriculum can be challenging, but exciting! It's important to focus on choosing the curriculum that will be the best fit for your family. Some families may need and prefer a more structured curriculum, while others will do best with more freedom in their curriculum and daily schedule.

In choosing a curriculum for my own child, I had to take a couple of things into consideration. We lived in New York, which is a state with lots of homeschooling regulations. Therefore, I needed to follow those guidelines. However, I couldn't do school-at-home during school hours, because I was working and going to graduate school at the same time I was homeschooling my child. My son loved play, nature, and the outdoors, so I needed to choose a curriculum that would involve some outdoor exploration. Finally, my son was super intrinsically moti-vated about topics he was interested in, so I wanted to preserve that excitement about learning. After a brief period of trying a more structured, state-based curriculum with not-so-wonderful results, an eclectic method of home learning, rooted in unschooling and the philosophy of romanticism, worked best for us.

It ends up we were in good company! Lots of home-schooling parents, including Ree Drummond (aka The Pioneer Woman), have chosen an eclectic, unstruc-tured approach. As Ree states in one of her 2017 blog postings:

> *When I first started out, the fear and uncertainty I felt about homeschooling caused me to go a little berserk. In preparation for that first year, I created an intricate color-coded chart that accounted for each and every thirty-minute time slot from 6 a.m. to 4 p.m. I followed my psychotic color-coded schedule to a T . . . for four days. Then I gave up. My goals are yearly these days. I know what grade my kids are in, what materials they'll need to attain a certain level of knowledge by the end of the year, and I jump in. Some days, I'm pleased with the amount of work we get done. Other days, we never look at a book because the kids are working cattle or I decide I can't be bothered with Advanced Physics . . .*

How to Create a Homeschool Schedule

Creating a homeschool schedule helps families organize and map out teaching goals. Some families create yearly schedules, while others create monthly, weekly, or daily schedules. You may need to vary the details in your homeschool schedule based on state regulations. You'll also want to consider the amount of structure that works best for you and your family. Whichever schedule format you choose, share the schedule frequently with your child or teen, so everyone is on the same page when it comes to home learning!

Yearly

A yearly schedule is especially helpful if you live in a state with high or moderate homeschool regulations, as your yearly schedule will be a part of the paperwork you submit to your state or district along with your chosen curriculum. A yearly schedule will outline all you want to get done in the year. This may include a list of the subjects and topics you'll cover, and the materials you'll choose. For example, I used a yearly template to document plans for my son's ninth grade year (see page 102).

Quarterly

Many school districts ask homeschooling parents to send in quarterly reports, in which case a quarterly schedule is helpful. When I was homeschooling, my quarterly schedule contained the topics and material to be covered, as well as a space for assessment, where I would review my son's progress in each subject at the end of the quarter. Again, the level of detail and structure may vary depending on what needs to be covered, your family's preferences, and other relevant considerations. (See an example of a quarterly schedule on page 102.)

Weekly

Weekly schedules are especially beneficial for homeschooling parents and students after they've made a yearly and quarterly schedule. Weekly schedules outline tasks and activities for the week in an easy-to-read format. When I homeschooled my son, I would keep our weekly schedule in an academic planner we could both access. You can also use a digital calendar or create your own calendar using the model below. Weekly schedules can be filled in on Sunday and used throughout the week. This can be especially helpful to keep track of progress and to refer to as needed during the week, facilitating a clear sense of learning goals for both parent and child. You'll also find it helpful to refer to this weekly schedule when you have to document your child's learning for your state or district. (See an example of a weekly schedule using the eclectic method on page 108.)

Block

Block schedules are frequently used in middle and high schools, and they may be relevant for older homeschoolers who want to spend expanded time during the day on one subject or one activity. Block schedules are also helpful for homeschooling parents who need to coordinate their own schedules with a schedule for their child. In addition, home learners who thrive with a strong sense of structure may prefer this method as it clearly outlines days and times for designated activities. Within a block schedule, each subject is not done every day. Instead, a subject is covered two or three times per week. Time is blocked out for specific subjects or activities. (See a sample block schedule on page 110.)

Loop

Think of a loop schedule as a rotating to-do list for home learning. Basically, in a loop schedule you make a list of everything your child needs to cover during the day, in an order you and your child agree on. Then, your child starts at the top of the list and moves through each subject in order. On the next day, you pick up wherever you stopped on the previous day. Eventually, you reach the end of the list and begin again. This approach is ideal for those who want a pre-determined structure for each day while also allowing for freedom, choice, and autonomy.

For example, our homeschool loop would look like this:

1. English language arts

2. History

3. Biology

4. Algebra

5. Physical and health education

6. Music

7. Art

8. Foreign language

Loop schedules are helpful for those who like lists, as well as those who like to spend unlimited time on specific subjects. On a typical day, you may go through four or five subjects. However, on some days, you may cover only one or two subjects, and that is just fine!

YEARLY HOMESCHOOL SCHEDULE TEMPLATE

Subject	ENGLISH LANGUAGE ARTS	HISTORY	BIOLOGY	ALGEBRA
Topics to be covered				
Materials to be used				

QUARTERLY HOMESCHOOL SCHEDULE EXAMPLE

SUBJECT	Topics to be covered	Materials to be used
LANGUAGE ARTS	• Grade-level reading • Use of quotation marks and capitalization • Daily vocabulary review • Frequent writing of essays and stories • Frequent reading of fiction and nonfiction books and magazines	• The Wizard of Earthsea by Ursula LeGuin • Animal Farm by George Orwell • To Kill a Mockingbird by Harper Lee • Journal for writing • Vocabulary cards
HISTORY	• Colonial ways of life • The American Revolution • Creating a Constitution • Federalists • The young republic • The idea of manifest destiny • The Civil War and Reconstruction	• History textbook • The New York Times

HEALTH AND PHYSICAL EDUCATION	MUSIC	ART	FOREIGN LANGUAGE

Assessment

Ben, being the voracious reader that he is, enjoyed two out of the three books he was assigned for required reading. Animal Farm *and* The Wizard of Earthsea *were his favorites.* The Wizard of Earthsea *reminded Ben of the J. R. R. Tolkien series* The Lord of the Rings, *and he frequently compared and contrasted the two (both in writing and discussion). I am truly impressed with the progress Ben has made in writing and grammar. To watch him write, freely and without prodding, has been a joy. Satisfactory progress has been made in all areas.*

Ben truly enjoys reading his textbook, The American Vision. *It gives him deep understanding and exposure to the history of our country and the birth of modern America. In our home, history works best when it is living history, and we feel lucky to be near so many wonderful historical resources and landmarks. Daily reading of* The New York Times *brings past and present to our living room every morning. Satisfactory progress has been made in all areas.*

CONTINUED >>

SUBJECT	Topics to be covered	Materials to be used
BIOLOGY	• Gregor Mendel: The science of heredity • Intro to DNA/double helix • Ecosystems • The water cycle • Biological communities • The environment • Plants and plant reproduction • The human brain exhibit at the Museum of Natural History	• Biology textbook • Field trips • Science Times
ALGEBRA	• Circumference and area • Order of operations • Evaluation of algebraic expressions • Exponents • Measures of central tendency • Inequalities • Graphical solutions of inequalities • Intro to geometric solids	• Math textbook • Math for Everyday Life

Ben worked really hard in biology this quarter. Through readings, videos, and real-world experiments, Ben came to appreciate the fact that biology is truly the study of life. The water cycle and plant reproduction were particularly interesting to Ben. The human brain exhibit at the American Museum of Natural History was truly amazing, and Ben and I had a great time exploring the permanent exhibits on different parts of the ecosystem there. Satisfactory progress has been made in all areas.

I am really proud of the work Ben has been doing in algebra. Ben enjoys the language of numbers, and has had great success in memorization of formulas and applying math concepts to more complex problems. Ben especially enjoys using measures of central tendency (and applies them to his bowling and golf scores). Graphic inequalities seem to come easy to Ben and coordinate systems/graphics seem to be a strong point. We have just finished the Geometric Solids chapter in his algebra book, and Ben seems to have a good grasp of the topic. Satisfactory progress has been made in all areas.

CONTINUED >>

SUBJECT	Topics to be covered	Materials to be used
HEALTH AND PHYSICAL EDUCATION	• Dangers of drugs, alcohol, and tobacco • Fire prevention • Highway and safety rules • Importance of living a healthy life • Participation in a variety of indoor and outdoor sports • Participation in bowling league • Participation in golf lessons	• Visit to firehouse for Fire Safety Day
MUSIC	• Guitar and bass lessons • Jam band • Visit to theater	• Lessons and internet
ART	• Use of a wide variety of art techniques • Frequent visits to museums and art galleries	• Museums and art materials
FOREIGN LANGUAGE	• Continuing German language studies	• German language app

Satisfactory progress has been made in all areas.

Satisfactory progress has been made in all areas.

Satisfactory progress has been made in all areas.

Satisfactory progress has been made in all areas.

WEEKLY HOMESCHOOL SCHEDULE EXAMPLE

	Monday	*Tuesday*
ENGLISH LANGUAGE ARTS	*Read last chapter of* The Wizard of Earthsea	*Compare* The Wizard of Earthsea *with* The Lord of the Rings *(in writing)*
HISTORY	*Discuss the American Revolution*	*Watch some of* Hamilton
BIOLOGY	*Cell biology*	*Create model of cell*
ALGEBRA	*Order of operations/ PEMDAS*	*Review PEMDAS*
PHYSICAL EDUCATION	*Bowling*	*Golf*
MUSIC	*Practice guitar*	*Practice guitar*
ART	*Review of famous artwork using art postcard*	*Visit Edward Hopper's house*
FOREIGN LANGUAGE	*20 minutes of German on app*	*20 minutes of German on app*

Wednesday	Thursday	Friday
Vocabulary review	Grammar review	Free-write essay, read The New York Times
Finish Hamilton	Research the Federalist Papers	Visit copy of Federalist Papers at local library
Discuss genetics	Read collected articles about genetics	Discuss Watson and Crick with Poppy
Apply PEMDAS to mathematical equations	More PEMDAS practice	Visit the bank, add to savings, discuss compound interest
Walk/run	Golf	Walk/run
Guitar lesson	Practice guitar	Jam band
Draw/create	Draw/create	Attend Picasso lecture at library
20 minutes of German on app	20 minutes of German on app	20 minutes of German on app

BLOCK HOMESCHOOL SCHEDULE EXAMPLE

	Monday	*Tuesday*
8–9 a.m.	*Wake up/ morning chores*	*Wake up/ morning chores*
9–11 a.m.	*Math*	*History or science*
Noon–1 p.m.	*Lunch and reading or walk*	*Lunch and reading or walk*
1–3 p.m.	*Trip, writing, or exploration of special topic*	*Trip, writing, or exploration of special topic*
3–5:30 p.m.	*English language arts*	*Math*
5:30–7 p.m.	*Dinner*	*Dinner*
7–9 p.m.	*Sports activity, music practice, or German*	*Sports activity, music practice, or German*
9 p.m.	*Quiet activity before bed*	*Quiet activity before bed*

Wednesday	Thursday	Friday
Wake up/ morning chores	Wake up/ morning chores	Wake up/ morning chores
Math	History or science	Math/English language arts or special project
Lunch and reading or walk	Lunch and reading or walk	Lunch and reading or walk
Trip, writing, or exploration of special topic	Trip, writing, or exploration of special topic	Trip, writing, or exploration of special topic
English language arts	Math	Health or art
Dinner	Dinner	Dinner
Sports activity, music practice, or German	Sports activity, music practice, or German	Sport activity or music practice/ jam band
Quiet activity before bed	Quiet activity before bed	Quiet activity before bed

Daily

When I homeschooled my son, a daily schedule worked best for us, given my variable work schedule and the eclectic model of homeschooling we used. You might like to use a daily schedule in conjunction with yearly, quarterly, and weekly schedules to organize and structure your child's home learning. It's helpful to post your daily schedule on an electronic calendar or to print and post it on a fridge or desk for reference. An example of our daily schedule is below.

MONDAY	Activity
8–9 a.m.	Wake up/morning chores
9–noon	Reading, math, writing, and review of core subject of choice
Noon–1 p.m.	Lunch/walk/play
1–3 p.m.	Field trip or core subject work
3–4 p.m.	Outside chores/use of core subjects in everyday life
4–5:30 p.m.	Extracurricular activity
5:30–7 p.m.	Dinner, then reading or walk

7-9 p.m.	*Sports, music lessons, language learning, or drawing*
9-10 p.m.	*Quiet activity before bed (usually reading, games, or watching a TV show together)*

A Guide to Standardized Testing

While standardized testing is not required in all states, it can help homeschooling families assess progress and prepare for higher-stakes testing like the SAT and ACT. Standardized testing can also help assure homeschooling families that the learner is working at a typical grade level when compared with traditionally schooled peers. Whether you use standardized testing really depends on your state's homeschooling laws and the homeschooling model or philosophy you've chosen.

State Standardized Testing

Many states require homeschoolers to submit standardized test scores after each year of homeschooling is completed, usually toward the end of the school year. Check your state homeschool regulations to see if standardized testing is required for your child or teen. Most districts will send state homeschool regulations after they receive and process your letter of intent to homeschool. You can also look up regulations on your state education department's website or search the state-by-state regulation listing at HSLDA.org/legal.

States that require students to take standardized tests generally give options for what particular test your child can take and for how that test can be administered and scored. Do your research and make sure you choose the test (and administration options) that will work best for your own family situation. Below you'll find a summary of the different standardized tests that states often recommend.

The Iowa Test of Basic Skills

The Iowa Test of Basic Skills (ITBS) assesses students in kindergarten through 12th grade on all major subjects, including reading, English language arts, math, science, and social studies. Depending on grade level, the test contains 270 to 340 questions, and takes 3 to 3½ hours to complete. The ITBS is given individually by a certified test administrator, although it can also be taken in a group format in either a school or home environment. Parents can register to be a test administrator if they have a bachelor's degree or above. The ITBS can be given and then sent to a registered testing group for scoring. Students who would like to get used to the format of the ITBS can find practice tests available for purchase on the Mercer Publishing website (MercerPublishing.com).

The Stanford Achievement Test

The Stanford Achievement Test is considered to be the most rigorous of all the major achievement tests. It assesses students in kindergarten through 12th grade on all core subjects, including reading comprehension, math, science, and social studies. The test itself is untimed. It can usually be completed in 2½ to 5 hours. The Stanford Achievement Test can be administered by a test administrator in a home or school. It can also be taken online with a proctor's assistance via phone. Parents can register to be a test administrator if they have a bachelor's degree or above. Free sample test questions and sample Stanford Achievement Test reports can be found on the Pearson test website (PearsonAssessments.com).

THE CALIFORNIA ACHIEVEMENT TEST

The California Achievement Test is considered the easiest of the major achievement tests and can be obtained through BJU Press (BJUPress.com) or Christian Liberty Press (Shop ChristianLiberty.com). It assesses students in grades 4 through 12 on skills in reading, English language arts, and math. It takes approximately 2½ hours to administer. The California Achievement Test has no specific administration criteria requirements. It can be administered by a parent at home; no bachelor's degree required. Sample California Achievement Test questions can be found in the book *Spectrum Test Practice Reproducible*, which can be purchased through SetonTesting.com.

THE PERSONALIZED ASSESSMENT OF STUDENT SUCCESS

The Personalized Assessment of Student Success (PASS) test is the assessment I used when testing my son. The PASS test is popular among homeschooling families because it's an untimed test. It contains a pretest that students take to determine the most appropriate level of test to administer in reading, math, and English language arts. This pretest acknowledges that not all students in the same grade are at the same level of academic skill. The PASS test is appropriate for students in grades 3 through 8, and it's been approved in the states of New York, North Carolina, Washington, and Alaska as a test for state reporting. School districts in other states may accept the PASS test, too, but you should gain approval from your district before using it as an official assessment. The PASS can be administered by a parent at home, although it can also be administered in a group setting. The PASS test can be purchased through Hewitt Learning (HewittLearning.org) and is scored by the same company.

The Scholastic Aptitude Test

The Scholastic Aptitude Test (SAT) measures a student's readiness or capability for learning in a college environment. The test itself is an important option for homeschoolers to consider, as it may boost a homeschooler's transcript or portfolio and some colleges require the SAT for admissions.

The SAT is offered six times a year, at local high schools throughout the country. Students usually take this test when they're in grades 10 through 12. The test itself is strictly proctored. It contains three major components: a reading section, a writing/language section, and a math section. Within the reading section, students are asked to read passages and interpret informational graphics, testing a student's knowledge of collecting evidence and context clues and their knowledge of history, social studies, and science. The writing section focuses on a student's proofreading and editing skill sets, asking test takers to read passages and find errors in them. The math section is heavy on problem-solving skills, algebraic skills, math tool/calculator use, and real-world application.

The SAT is given by a company called The College Board (CollegeReadiness.CollegeBoard.org/sat). You'll find it helpful to consult The College Board's website for more information about the test and to review sample test questions. Sample questions and tests are also available in test prep books that can be purchased in local bookstores or online. You may also find these at local libraries. Many test preparation centers, like The Princeton Review or Kaplan, offer SAT test prep courses for a significant price (usually between $1,000 and $2,000).

ACT

The ACT (originally called American College Testing) is another test that measures a student's readiness or capability for learning in a college environment. The ACT is accepted as a substitute for the SAT at most colleges and universities across the United States. It's offered four to six times a year at high schools and college testing centers. Like the SAT, it is usually taken by students in grades 10 through 12 and it's formally proctored.

The ACT contains four major components: a reading section, a writing section, a math section, and a science section. The ACT reading section contains 40 questions that must be answered within a 35-minute time limit. The questions are based on passages chosen from the social sciences, humanities, and sciences. The ACT writing section is a 75-minute, 45-question test that measures skills of grammar, knowledge of language, and organization of writing. The math section of the ACT is 60 questions (to be answered in 60 minutes) and is focused on geometry, algebra, and trigonometry. The science section is 40 questions (to be answered in 35 minutes) and concentrates on the comprehension of science passages and general science knowledge.

The ACT is given by the American College Testing Service (ACT.org). Students and parents can consult the website for more information about the test, sample test questions, and registration information. ACT test prep books are also helpful resources. You can find them at libraries and bookstores throughout the United States. Test prep centers such as Princeton Review and Kaplan also offer structured ACT prep courses for an approximate cost of $1,500.

How to Record Homeschool Grades

For some, grades are a practical way to measure homeschool goals and assess assignments, tests, projects, and quizzes. For others, grades are required by law under state homeschooling regulations. Grades can also be a form of documentation that may be helpful later if your child decides to attend a college or university that prefers formal, grade-based homeschool transcripts. Some students find grades motivating and want grades to be part of their homeschooling experience. If you decide to formally grade your homeschooled student, there are different ways to do so.

How to Calculate Percentage and Letter Grades

Some families, especially those doing a school-at-home model, decide that percentage and letter grades are best, because they replicate the way schools formally assess students. Most schools use a 100-point scale in terms of grading, with letter grades that correspond to a specific percentage of 100. The table below shows the grading criteria schools typically use. You can use it within your homeschool environment as well.

Performance Indicator	Percentage Point	Letter Grade
Highly exceptional	100 – 97.5%	A+
Outstanding	97.4 – 92.5%	A
Excellent	92.4 – 90.0%	A-
Very good	89.9 – 87.5%	B+
Good	87.4 – 82.5%	B
Acceptable	82.4 – 80.0%	B-
Fair	79.9 – 77.5%	C+
Minimally acceptable	77.4 – 70.0%	C
Work only completed	69.9 – 66%	D
Failure	65% and under	F

How to Calculate a Grade Point Average

Some institutions go one step further and provide numeric equivalents to convert letter grades into a numeric value out of 4.0. Colleges and universities throughout the country use this grade point average (GPA) method, and so do some private and public high schools. As a homeschooling family, you can use it as well. Below you can find a chart of percentage point scores, letter grades, and their GPA equivalents.

Percentage Point	Letter Grade	Grade Point Average
100 - 97.5%	A+	4.0
97.4 - 92.5%	A	4.0
92.4 - 90.0%	A-	3.7
89.9 - 87.5%	B+	3.3
87.4 - 82.5%	B	3.0
82.4 - 80.0%	B-	2.7
79.9 - 77.5%	C+	2.3
77.4 - 70.0%	C	2.0
69.9 - 66%	D	1.0
65% and under	F	0

Although some homeschool families use grades, others may not. If your state does not require the use of grades as assessment criteria, you can choose to write a qualitative summary of student progress. This qualitative summary should contain a review of work completed during the academic quarter or year, with a paragraph or two outlining the specific progress made, student strengths, and what the student will continue to work on. Qualitative summaries sometimes give more information than a letter grade or GPA ever would, and some districts prefer them.

How to Teach with Video Games and Interactive Media

Video games and other interactive media can be great teaching tools! They help students develop hand-eye coordination and refine small motor skills. They also improve attention, memory, and decision-making skills. Many children and teens who engage in video game play eventually become interested in programming, coding, and computer-aided design. Evolutionary psychologist Dr. Peter Gray, in his blog *Freedom to Learn*, frequently posts about the cognitive and emotional benefits of video games. Video games are especially popular with homeschoolers and their parents, who have realized the many benefits of specific games to enhance home learning skills.

Video Games

» Minecraft (Minecraft.net) is the best-selling video game of all time. It's a block-based, three-dimensional world in which participants can discover and extract raw materials, craft tools and useful items, and learn how to build structures. Many homeschoolers play Minecraft. In fact, one of my colleagues has created a university-based Minecraft club, open to college students and a home learning group. Together, this group has created a model of Mars, along with structures and tools that allow their Minecraft characters to survive on the planet. This model of Mars also assists learners in studying the unique topography of the planet, giving them specific science knowledge.

» BrainHQ (BrainHQ.com) offers fun online games that focus on increasing attention, brain speed, memory, people skills, navigation, and intelligence. The games are appropriate for children and adults alike. You can find BrainHQ in both free and paid versions. The neurobiological benefits of using this video game have been well researched and verified by hundreds of academic studies.

» Math Blaster (MathBlaster.com) is the most popular set of math games on the internet. Math Blaster allows an individual to customize an avatar and explore an intergalactic world where players can learn math and science facts. There are many fun games and activities on this site. MathBlaster.com also contains a section called Cool Math that includes math tips, worksheets, and math activities. Math Blaster is most appropriate for kids in kindergarten through eighth grades.

Television and Movies

Some students are more visual learners, and movies and clips of movies can be helpful learning tools for them. As a home-schooling mom, I frequently used video clips to explain a difficult concept or to preview a book or period we were studying. Sometimes, it was a movie that got us more interested in a book (*To Kill a Mockingbird* is one example), and other times, we would read a book (like *Harry Potter and the Sorcerer's Stone*) and then want to watch the movie. We rarely watched movies in theaters. Instead, we borrowed DVDs from our local library, or watched clips on YouTube.

» Streaming movies can get expensive, especially when using streaming services that charge a monthly fee. Recently, my son and I have gotten into watching documentaries and short films on Kanopy (Kanopy.com), a free movie streaming service we have access to via our local library. Kanopy has many incredible educational documentary and film selections. They also have a great selection of cartoons and shows for younger children.

» Public television is also having a huge resurgence thanks to this era of increased home learning. Stations across the country run a PBS KIDS 24/7 channel for children ages two to eight, filled with curriculum-based content and fun educational shows, including the beloved *Sesame Street*. PBS also runs a free livestream through

PBSKids.org. Many states are also providing a "Learn at Home" series through public television for students in kindergarten through 12th grades. Look up your local television listings for details or consult the American Public Television Station website at APTS.org.

Social Media

When I was homeschooling my son, Facebook and Twitter existed, but they weren't as popular as they are now. We didn't really use social media except to connect with family and friends who lived far away. My son didn't get a cell phone until he started driving at age 16, and still, as an adult, only uses his phone for business, phone calls, and internet surfing. I probably use my phone (and social media) twice as much as he does.

We tend to complain when our children or teens spend too much time on their phones. However, social media sites can serve as good learning tools, as long as they're properly used. It's important to have frequent discussions with your learner about responsible social media use and to model the principles you teach.

» Facebook Youth Portal (https://www.facebook.com /safety/youth) is a site that shows teenagers how to responsibly use Facebook for discussion and advocacy. It's especially important that your child or teen read through this site prior to joining Facebook, as they should be aware of ways to be accountable for their social media use, as well as how to use social media for positive purposes.

» Twitter is a great way to connect with politicians, favorite celebrities, and authors. It's also a fun place for parents and teens to have conversations about homeschooling with others who are also home learning. Popular homeschool hashtags on Twitter include:

#homeschooling, #homeschool, #homeschoollife, #homeschoolmom, #homeeducation, #learningthroughplay, #learningathome, #unschooling, #homeschoolers, #homeschoolfamily, #stayhome, and #homeschooler.

» I've known several teens who have created professional portfolios of their art, dance, music, craft, or athletic accomplishments through Instagram. Instagram allows users to post pictures and short videos, and it is a perfect medium for portfolio work and personal connection.

» TikTok can be a wonderful resource for quick how-to videos. Using TikTok, I have learned how to make healthy meals, use American Sign Language, and learned about financial strategies, too. Many teens have used TikTok to learn dance moves and drawing techniques, and to create short videos of their own.

Interactive Video

» You can create an entire homeschool curriculum using content from Khan Academy (KhanAcademy.org). Its mission is to create free, accessible, world-class pre-K through 12th grade video-based curricula—and it really does a wonderful job of that. Students can learn math, science, reading, English language arts, history, humanities, economics, computing, and life skills through Khan Academy videos. There are also ACT and SAT prep videos on the site. Teachers commonly use Khan Academy to introduce topics in their classrooms, and homeschooling parents can do the same.

» BrainPop.com is an incredible, interactive video-based website for students from kindergarten through grade 12. BrainPop contains in-depth content on math, English, science, social studies, arts and music, health, social emotional learning, and engineering and technology. It also contains content on new and trending ideas in politics, health, and education. Each topic includes an interactive video, graphic organizers, subject-based vocabulary, worksheets, related readings, games, and ideas for creative projects. BrainPop charges a yearly subscription fee, which runs about $150 to $175.

» Flocabulary.com includes interactive, hip-hop inspired video content and instructional activities for students from kindergarten through grade 12. Subjects covered include English language arts, math, science, social studies, life skills, vocabulary, and current events. Parents who are homeschooling can gain access to Flocabulary Lite for free for 30 days. After that, there's a charge of $10 to $15 a month. This is worth it if your child likes modern, fun, hip-hop-based materials!

How to Manage Your Teaching Resources

Homeschooling is an amazing educational alternative! However, it does cost some money to do it well. Remember, I homeschooled my son as a single mother on a very strict budget, so I know firsthand that creating an incredible educational experience for your child with little or no money is possible. But it's crucial to consider potential expenses when thinking about and researching prospective teaching resources and learn how to navigate these expenses.

Most homeschoolers in 2021 need access to a computer, and they need reliable internet access. The least expensive way to go is to purchase a Google-based Chromebook, which will cost you about $300 to $500, and internet access in most areas is about $20 to $30 a month. If you fall into a low-income bracket, many internet providers may have free or lower-cost services available. All it takes is an ask. For example, AT&T offers Access from AT&T, which is an application-based, lower-cost internet service.

If you're using a pre-boxed curriculum, note that this will add to your homeschool expenses. However, using a purchased boxed or online curriculum program, especially if you live in a highly regulatory state, makes school district reporting much easier. Most curriculum companies offer a grade-based boxed or online curriculum for $500 to $800, including all necessary materials. But you don't need to purchase a curriculum to successfully homeschool. If you're utilizing a school-at-home model, you can collect all the materials you need from various websites, the local library, and a free video resource like Khan Academy.

Along with a computer and some sort of curriculum, you'll need to budget for school supplies like pens, pencils, markers, crayons, printer paper, and printer ink. Be sure to shop during late August sales at big-box office retailers, as this can save you a significant amount of money later. I used to get all our school supplies for the year in late August for less than $100, including notebooks, binders, and stickers.

Field trips are the best part of school and homeschool! I would budget $50 a month for each child for special trips, such as visits to museums, historical houses, or theaters. You'll also find many opportunities to take free field trips wherever you live! As mentioned earlier, most museums, zoos, historical houses, and music venues have free days when you and your family can visit at no charge. You can also purchase a one-time subscription to a museum, zoo, or historical house, allowing you time to really explore the place in multiple trips. Also, remember that state and local parks are free and provide amazing outdoor experiences for your child or teen.

Subscriptions can come in other forms, too. We always subscribed to one newspaper and one magazine when my son was homeschooling. The newspaper allowed us to discuss current events together, and it was something we would both wake up and read, giving us some quiet morning time. The magazine subscription was usually related to a hobby. For example, when my son was interested in golf, he was gifted a subscription to *Golf Digest.* When he got into guitar, he started subscribing to *Guitar Player* magazine. If your child enjoys visual media, this category could include subscriptions to streaming services like Netflix or Hulu and to educational sites like BrainPop or Flocabulary.

Extracurricular activities are an additional expense. However, if you can afford to give your child access to a hobby or sport they love, they'll reap the rewards later. Participation in music, dance, theater, and sports can lead to feelings of mastery (and maybe even college scholarships!). It can also allow your child a dedicated space to make lifelong friendships. Extracurriculars are not always expensive. Our local library offers free weekly courses in origami, knitting, and chess, and our community center offers low-cost arts-and-crafts classes and sports leagues. Boy Scouts, Girl Scouts, Boys & Girls Clubs, and 4-H are also free or low cost to join and provide kids and teens with a variety of activities.

Create a Homeschool Resource Management Plan

You can use a simple homeschool resource management plan to categorize, allocate, and manage resources for homeschooling. This plan will help you budget homeschool expenses for the year. An example plan is below. Note that if your child went to a physical school, you would need and use most of these resources anyway, with the exception of curricula, materials, and extra funding for field trips. Unfortunately, home learning expenses are not tax deductible in most states (Illinois, Louisiana, and Minnesota are the only states that currently allow tax credits for homeschooling families). But if you also keep a home office, you may be able to deduct items like computers, internet access, printer paper, and printer cartridges.

Item	Description	Cost Per Year
Computer	Chromebook	$500 (this is a one-time expenditure)
Internet access	Internet/phone carrier	$250
Materials	Boxed curriculum with materials	$800
School supplies	Pencils, pens, markers, printer paper and ink	$250
Field trips	Museums, zoos, historical houses, parks (including food)	$600
Subscriptions	Newspapers, streaming services, and apps	$400
Extracurricular activities	Music lessons and sports fees	$1,000 (optional)

Where to Find Reliable Teaching Resources

Just as our children and teens need to know how to find reliable resources for papers and projects, homeschooling parents need to know where to find trustworthy teaching resources. The list below outlines only a few free resources, but I hope, after you read this book, you'll collect more resources as you move forward in your homeschooling journey!

» The University at Albany has created RemoteED, an internet resource for homeschooling parents and educators. RemoteED (AATLASed.org) contains a comprehensive listing of curriculum-based materials for students from kindergarten through grade 12, organized by subject and grade. RemoteED also hosts weekly professional development seminars called "Community Conversations" on writing, organization, and self-care that homeschooling parents are invited to be a part of.

» For those interested in STEM fields, NASA.gov has an amazing collection of materials for home learners. NASA at Home contains free e-books, videos, games, virtual tours, and podcasts on the topics of space, aeronautics, planets, and galaxies.

» Project Gutenberg (Gutenberg.org) is a library of more than 60,000 free e-books. All the world's greatest literature is found in digital form on Project Gutenberg, especially classical works. Popular titles include *Pride and Prejudice* by Jane Austen, *The Scarlet Letter* by Nathaniel Hawthorne, and *A Tale of Two Cities* by Charles Dickens.

» Education.com contains the most comprehensive collection of downloadable worksheets for kids in pre-K through 6th grade, including students who are English language learners. The worksheets and activities on Education.com are easy to download, and they align with Common Core Learning Standards. Common Core Learning Standards are grade- and subject-based goals for math and English language arts that are shared by most states.

CHAPTER TEN

CREATE A HOMESCHOOL LESSON PLAN

Writing lesson plans requires time, dedication, and a keen understanding of student abilities and goals. Not every homeschooling family writes or prepares lesson plans. Unschoolers or those who are using a more unstructured homeschooling model generally don't plan structured lessons. But some homeschoolers depend on specific subject lesson plans to keep them organized and on track.

For example, one homeschooling parent I know is a former public school teacher who currently owns a successful tutoring business. For her, lesson planning for her own children is completed on Sunday evenings, just like she would complete lesson plans for her class at school. She keeps her lesson plans organized in a binder and reflects on each lesson afterward, specifically writing down what worked within the lesson and what did not. She'll also note on her lesson plans if her children applied what they learned to real-world situations. She creates lesson plans for each specific subject, including extras like music, art, foreign language, and physical education. Lesson planning is what works for her.

What Is a Lesson Plan?

A lesson plan is a detailed outline that helps teachers break down new concepts into practical learning steps for students. Before creating a lesson for a student, ask yourself the following questions:

» What is the topic I'm focusing this lesson on?

» What is the primary purpose or goal of the lesson?

» What resources and materials do I need to teach the lesson?

» How do the activities draw on the strengths, needs, and interests of the learner?

» How can the lesson I'm teaching be generalized to the real world?

You should be very clear regarding the goal of the lesson, because if you aren't clear, your child won't be either. The materials and resources you choose should be topic specific, but should also draw on the strengths, needs, and interests of the learner. For example, if you know your child is a visual learner, integrate video clips and visuals into your lesson. If your child is an auditory learner, audiobooks and podcasts are helpful to include in your lesson. If your child is a kinesthetic learner, make sure the lesson you're planning incorporates some sort of movement.

In terms of resources and materials, you can use the textbooks you've purchased or items from your boxed curriculum, but don't forget all the free resources you can also integrate (see chapter 9). Finally, you want to think about generalization—that is, how the lesson you're teaching your child can be generalized to real-world learning or generalized to later learning in high school and college. When I instruct public school teachers, I always say, "If the lesson can't be generalized to your students' everyday lives, then you may want to think twice about teaching the lesson." Education should be focused on preparing children and teens for the real world.

How to Create a Lesson Plan

A simple lesson plan should be broken down into specific parts:

» First, you'll find it helpful to think of a title for your lesson, or you can just write down the specific topic you want to teach.

» Then, you want to think of the purpose or goal of your lesson. What do you want your student to get out of the lesson?

» Next come the materials or resources needed to teach the lesson. These can be textbooks, worksheets, articles or resources from the internet, and online games. You can also include writing-based materials like pens and pencils, graph paper, or a lined notebook.

» Finally, think of how your lesson will draw on the strengths, needs, and interests of your learner, as well as how the lesson can be generalized to the real world or future learning in high school or college.

Now you're ready to write the actual lesson! I liked to break my lessons down into periods. For example, I would review a concept related to the lesson for 5 minutes. For the next 15 minutes, we'd watch a Khan Academy or BrainPop video on the lesson. After that, I used 10 minutes for direct instruction on the topic, and another 15 minutes for my child to try out what he'd learned. I also left time at the end of the lesson to answer any questions my son had on the material, or to assess him on his understanding of the lesson in some way.

After I taught the lesson, or in the evening, I spent some specific time reflecting on the lesson. I asked myself three questions:

» What elements of the lesson worked well?

» What did not?

» How can I specifically improve on subsequent lessons in order to best meet the needs of my child?

EXAMPLE *Lesson Plan*

Below is an example of a homeschool lesson plan. This particular lesson was focused on the skeletal system. Note that the lesson had a clear goal and really took into consideration the learner's strengths and learning preferences. The lesson itself was also highly generalizable to real life.

Title of lesson: The Skeletal System

Learning goal/outcomes: Today we'll explore the structure and function of the skeletal system, including joints and bones.

Instructional materials/remote resources for lesson:

» Science textbook chapter 3
» Khan Academy video: KhanAcademy.org/science /high-school-biology/hs-human-body-systems /hs-the-musculoskeletal-system/v/skeletal -structure-and-function
» Image of skeletal system
» Bill Nye the Science Guy video on bones: YouTube.com /watch?v=KXqLr6TwPVA
» Skeletal system word search game

How do the activities draw on the strengths, needs, and interests of the learner? My son is a visual learner and enjoys videos and games. Two short videos will be shown during this lesson, and we'll culminate the lesson with a skeletal system word search.

How can the lesson be generalized to the real world? It's important for my son to know how the human body works so he can make choices to keep his body, bones, and joints in good health.

Estimated Time	Activity, Purpose, Instructional Materials	Ways to Check for Understanding, Teaching toward Independence
15 minutes	Review Khan Academy video on skeletal system Connect it to what we previously read in chapter 3 of science text	Watch video together Discussion-based check in
10 minutes	Use image of skeletal system to name common bones and learn how they are used Talk about the function of joints and how they hold bones together	Ben will use the image of the skeletal system to independently identify bones he knows.
20 minutes	Watch Bill Nye video on bones and joints, as Ben really likes Bill Nye	Ben will watch the video independently. At the end, I'll ask him to write down 3 things he learned about the video.
10 minutes	Complete skeletal system word search game	We'll do this for fun! Ben will start independently and together we'll complete the word search.

Reflection on the lesson: *(What happened after? What could be improved on/modified? What worked well?)* This lesson was great and Ben really enjoyed it. The Bill Nye video was long (20+ minutes), so I should have saved that for another lesson, especially since we'd already watched the Khan Academy video. Ben loved the word search and learned a lot from this lesson. He's excited to share his learning with his aunt who is a doctor.

I hope you find this reflection helpful! Try to always make some time to reflect on what worked and didn't work within a lesson after you've taught the lesson to your child. This will give you clues as to what works for your child moving forward, and it will help you structure additional homeschool lessons.

CHAPTER ELEVEN

PLANNING BEYOND YOUR FIRST HOMESCHOOL YEAR

Homeschooling is such an empowering experience for parents, students, families, and the communities that support them. Although my family, friends, and neighbors thought it was ridiculous when I chose to homeschool my son back in 2000, they later saw the benefits of a homeschooling environment. My parents now suggest home learning to their friends, and they are so proud of their grandson. Our neighbor, who was highly doubtful about home learning when we started, really appreciated how much Ben wanted to learn and how curious he was about everything. Ultimately, my neighbor said, "I am now a believer. Homeschooling really works." I'm especially appreciative of this particular neighbor, as he spent hours restoring a Ford Model T with my son, teaching him about mechanics, cars, and elements of engineering.

I'm also so grateful to our homeschooling support group, who encouraged us to continue homeschooling, even when it felt difficult. I was the only single parent in that group, and they nurtured me, gave me advice, and organized wonderful field trips that my son and I attended together. I still have such fond memories of Tuesday afternoon ice skating at a local state park, Thursday afternoon nature walks, and historic house tours on Friday morning with them.

When we were homeschooling, the community became our extended family. Because of homeschooling, we knew our grocer, banker, postman, and librarian. They watched my son grow up. They are almost as proud of him as I am. They frequently tell my son stories of how they remember us playing in the driveway in the middle of the day or how my son used to come to the bank on Fridays to deposit his allowance. He is still, to this day, a saver, and I love that the banker remembers him, even though my son is now an adult. The world was his classroom then, and still is now.

Empower Your Students to Take Charge

The narrative that surrounds every adult who was homeschooled is generally the same: a highly successful, highly educated, civically minded individual who is curious, self-directed, and entrepreneurial.

Academic preparedness is a strength in those who were home educated. Laurence Rudner of the University of Maryland gave achievement tests to 20,760 homeschooled students and found that they scored exceptionally high, within the 70th and 80th percentiles. Researchers have found that those who were homeschooled had higher ACT scores, GPAs, and graduation rates than their public school counterparts. Brian Ray, president of the National Home Education Research Institute, noted similar outcomes and believes the homeschooled student's strong ability to succeed in college comes from their self-discipline, motivation, self-direction, and initiative. In summary, experts say that homeschool graduates often outpace their peers in standardized testing, reading, writing, socialization, and civic engagement. They also graduate from college at a higher rate than their traditionally schooled peers.

What is the secret to the success of homeschooled learners? It's a combination of factors. First, homeschooling parents tend to be more involved in their child's educational endeavors. This is important because we know from research that high levels of parental involvement tend to lead to higher levels of academic achievement. Second, homeschoolers are not burnt out by school and they see learning as something they can do on their own. Homeschoolers recognize that they don't need to be in a classroom or at a computer all day to learn. Instead, they know that learning happens everywhere: indoors, outdoors, staying at home, or traveling. Third, and most important, homeschoolers tend to have high levels of intrinsic motivation. Instead of learning for the grade or for the test, homeschoolers learn because they want to and because they are interested in the topics they're studying. They don't have to stop learning when a class period ends or when the bell rings for dismissal. Instead, homeschoolers can take all the time they need to absorb material, observe, and make connections. That time is the biggest gift of home learning.

Here are some more tips for you at the beginning of your homeschooling journey:

» Allow your child or teen the time to explore during the home learning experience. Exploration leads to greater understanding, increased curiosity, and better critical thinking skills.

» Make room for change. If one homeschooling model is not working for your learner, feel free to move on to another model that may be a better fit.

» Give your child time to investigate their strengths, interests, and preferences, and assure children and teens that their choices matter. Support those choices and interests in every way you can.

» Take notes. Whether it is through journaling, scheduling, or lesson planning, document your child's first year homeschooling and beyond.

I still look back in awe on all the learning and growing Ben did each year. You'll do the same with your child.

Find a Homeschool Support Group

Education is as much an individual journey as it is a communal one. That's why I recommend you find a circle of support. Make sure both you and your child have people around you who support your homeschooling journey. If family and friends don't support your choice to homeschool, then find or create a homeschooling group that you can confide in and with whom your child or teen can have adventures.

You can first try to make personal connections with individuals in your community who have chosen home learning. They may know of or be involved in a local homeschool support group. If there is no one near you who homeschools, look to social media. Many homeschooling groups have a Facebook page or an Instagram account that is quite active and a great resource to new home learners. Blogs can also be a source of support. Early in our homeschooling years, I didn't have a local support group, but I read blogs of homeschooling parents, and those blogs were a source of great inspiration and community. In fact, I still keep in touch with many of those homeschooling moms whose blogs I read daily.

If there's no homeschooling group in your area, you can create one! Look for like-minded parents by making a Facebook group or putting up a flyer at a coffee shop or library. I used to host a homeschool support group right in my backyard. Although we were very different people, we all craved the same thing—reassurance and support—and our kids loved learning and playing together!

Whatever model or philosophy you and your family choose, I wish you all the best on your journey. I hope this guide was helpful in getting you started. Homeschooling is the most incredible experience, and one of the best decisions you can ever make for your child. Enjoy this precious time living and learning together!

FOR MORE
INFORMATION

The following resources have been essential to me as a homeschooling parent. I hope you find them helpful as well!

**Alternative Education Resource Organization.
EducationRevolution.org**
AERO was the first alternative education conference I ever attended.
The people at AERO always supported me in my path both as an
academic researcher and homeschooling mother. AERO's founder,
Jerry Mintz, is an icon within the alternative education realm. I highly
recommend this organization's yearly conference, as well as the infor-
mation contained within its website.

**Home School Legal Defense Association (HSLDA).
HSLDA.org/content**
The Home School Legal Defense Association supports the legal
rights of those who homeschool. It is an essential resource for all
homeschooling parents. The website also includes a state-by-state
summary of homeschooling regulations.

**Learning by Living. Spreaker.com/show/learning-by
-living-podcast**
A couple of years ago, Dr. Kevin Currie-Knight and I started a podcast focused on interviewing people within the homeschooling
and unschooling world. Later episodes of the podcast highlight the
accomplishments of those who have graduated from homeschooling
environments.

Life Learning Magazine. Life.ca/lifelearning

Founded by homeschooling parent Wendy Priesnitz in 2002, *Life Learning Magazine* features articles on topics relating to home-schooling, unschooling, and self-directed education. There is extensive information here for parents, children, families, and educators about how to get started on and thrive during your home learning journey.

Growing Without Schooling. JohnHoltGWS.com

Growing Without Schooling, created by John Holt and Pat Farenga, was the very first magazine focusing on the experiences of parents, children, and teens who engage in home education. Although it is no longer in print, it continues to be an important homeschooling resource.

Project World School. ProjectWorldSchool.com

For those who are interested in traveling while homeschooling, this is a website to explore. Project World School is the brainchild of Lainie Liberti and her son, Miro. The mission of Project World School is to provide international learning experiences for adolescents and young adults, with a strong emphasis on cooperative learning, co-creation, community, and social learning.

Sir Ken Robinson, "Do Schools Kill Creativity?" TED talk. TED.com/talks/sir_ken_robinson_do_schools_kill_creativity?language=en#t-2107

Sir Ken Robinson's famous TED talk has inspired so many educators, including home learners. A highly recommended watch!

**National Home Education Research Institute (NHERI).
NHERI.org**

NHERI is a source of research and support for both religious and secular home learners. I especially appreciate its focus on academic outcomes of those who have homeschooled, and its library of fact sheets for homeschooling parents.

REFERENCES

Bauer, S. W. & Wise, J. (2016). *The well-trained mind: A guide to classical education at home.* New York: W. W. Norton & Company.

Billings, L. (2016, June 10). "New map shows the dark side of artificial light at night." *Scientific American.* ScientificAmerican.com/article /new-map-shows-the-dark-side-of-artificial-light-at-night.

Blanding, M. (2018, October 2). "Twenty percent of home-schooled kids are getting 'unschooled'. What's that?" *The Boston Globe.* BostonGlobe.com/magazine/2018/10/02/home-schoolers-turn -boston-area-new-unschooling-centers/j4TB7K54hm7V7 riOyDPTIM/story.html.

Chase, S. & Morrison, K. (2018). "Implementation of multicultural education in unschooling and its potential." *International Journal of Multicultural Education, 20,* 39–58.

Cogan, M. (2010). "Exploring academic outcomes of homeschooled students." *The Journal of College Admission.* Files.Eric.gov /fulltext/EJ893891.pdf.

Cooper, B. S. & Sureau, J. (2007). "The politics of homeschooling: New developments, new challenges." *Educational Policy, 21*(1), 110–131.

Csoli, K. (2013). "Natural learning and learning disabilities: What I've learned as the parent of a 2 year old." *Journal of Unschooling and Alternative Learning, 7,* 92–104.

Davies, D., Jindal-Snape, D., Collier, C., Digby, R., Hay, P., Howe, A. (2013). "Creative learning environments in education—A systematic literature review." *Thinking Skills and Creativity, 8,* 80–91.

Deci, E. L. & Ryan, R. M. (1985). *Intrinsic motivation and self-determination in human behavior.* New York: Plenum Press.

Deci, E. L. & Ryan, R. M. (2008). "Facilitating optimal motivation and psychological well-being across life's domains." *Canadian Psychology, 49*(1), 14–23.

Deci, E. L. & Ryan, R. (2009). "Self-determination theory: A consideration of human motivation universals." In P. J. Corr & G. Matthews (Eds.), *The Cambridge Handbook of Personality Psychology* (441–456). New York: Cambridge University Press.

Deci, E. L. Vallerand, R. J., Pelletier, L. G., Ryan, R. M. (1991). "Motivation and education: The self-determination perspective." *Educational Psychologist, 26,* 325–346.

Dewey, J. (1916). *Democracy and education: An introduction to the philosophy of education.* New York: Macmillan.

Dewey, J. (1929). *My Pedagogic Creed.* Washington D.C.: The Progressive Education Association.

Dodd, S. (2019). "Sandra Dodd." SandraDodd.com.

Donnelly, M. (2016). "The human right of home education." *Journal of School Choice, 10,* 283–296.

Drummond, R. (2007). "Confessions of a pioneer woman: The relaxed homeschooler." ThePioneerWoman.com/homeschooling/the -relaxed-homeschooler.

Gray, P. (2013). *Free to learn: Why unleashing the instinct to play will make our children happier, more self-reliant, and better students for life.* New York: Basic Books.

Farenga, P. (2016). "The foundations of unschooling." JohnHoltGWS .com/the-foundations-of-unschooling.

Farenga, P. (2018–present). "Pat Farenga's blog." JohnHoltGWS.com.

Fensham-Smith, A. (2019). "Becoming a home educator in a networked world: Towards the democratisation of educational alternatives?" *Other Education*, 8, 27–57.

Fields-Smith, C. & Williams, M. R. (2009). "Sacrifices, challenges and empowerment: Black parents' decisions to home school." *Urban Review*, 41, 369–389.

Fields-Smith, C. & Kisura, M. W. (2013). "Resisting the status quo: The narratives of black homeschoolers in metro Atlanta and metro DC." *Peabody Journal of Education*, 88, 265–283.

Friend, M. (2013). *Special education: Contemporary perspectives for school professionals*. New York: Pearson Education.

Fuglei, M. (2015, January 21). "Unschooling: Inspirational learning method or educational neglect?" https://resilienteducator.com/classroom-resources/unschooling/

Gaither, M. (2018). *Homeschool: An American history*. New York: Palgrave Macmillan.

Gaither, M. (2018). "John Holt: American teacher and writer." *Encyclopedia Britannica*. Britannica.com/biography/John-Holt.

Gallup. (2020). *COVID–19 tracking poll, July 30-August 12, 2020* [data set]. Gallup Poll Social Series: Work and Education.

Gray, P. (2008–present). "Freedom to learn." *Psychology Today*. PsychologyToday.com/us/blog/freedom-learn.

Gray, P. & Riley, G. (2013). "The challenges and benefits of unschooling according to 232 families who have chosen that route." *Journal of Unschooling and Alternative Learning*, 7, 1–27.

Gray, P. & Riley, G. (2015). "Grown unschoolers' evaluations of their unschooling experience: Report I on a survey of 75 unschooled adults." *Other Education, 4*, 8–32.

Halpert, J. (2018, June 5). "Fostering connections between young and old." *The New York Times.* NYTimes.com/2018/06/05/well/family /elderly-loneliness-aging-intergenerational-programs-.html.

Hanes, S. (2016, February 14). "Free range education: Why the unschooling movement is growing." *The Christian Science Monitor.* CSMonitor.com/USA/Education/2016/0214/Free-range -education-Why-the-unschooling-movement-is-growing.

Hennessey, M. (2015, Summer). "Homeschooling in the city: Frustrated with public schools, middle class urbanites embrace an educational movement." *City Journal.* City-Journal.org/html /homeschooling-city-13742.html.

Hirsch Jr., E. D., ed. (2008–2013). *The core knowledge series.* New York: Penguin Random House.

Huseman, J. (2015, February 17). "The rise of the African American homeschoolers." *The Atlantic.* TheAtlantic.com/education /archive/2015/02/the-rise-of-homeschooling-among-black -families/385543.

Jackson, D. (2012, February 21). "Muslim families turn to home Schooling." *The Washington Times.* WashingtonTimes.com /news/2012/feb/21/muslim-families-turn-to-home-schooling.

Jones, P. & Gloeckner, G. (2004). "A study of college admissions officers' perceptions of and attitudes towards homeschooled students." *Journal of College Admission, 185*, 12–29.

Kunzman, R. (2017). "Homeschooler socialization: Skills, values, citizenship." In *The Wiley Handbook of Home Education*, M. Gaither (Ed.). Hoboken, NJ: John Wiley & Sons.

Lips, D. & Feinberg, E. (2008, April 3). "Homeschooling: A growing option in American Education." The Heritage Foundation. Heritage.org/education/report/homeschooling-growing-option-american-education.

Lyon, R. (2017, September 27). "NCES homeschooling data: First look." *International Center for Home Education Research Reviews.* ICHER.org/blog/?p=3906.

McQuiggan, M., Megra, M., Grady, S. (2017). *Parent and family involvement in education: Results from the National Household Education Surveys program of 2016.* Washington D.C.: The National Center for Education Statistics.

Medlin, R. G. (2006). "Homeschooled children's social skills." *Home School Researcher,* 17, 1–8.

Miltner, O. (2018, March 22). "The new face of U.S. homeschooling is Hispanic." OZY.com/fast-forward/the-new-face-of-u-s-homeschooling-is-hispanic/85278.

Montes, G. (2015). "The social and emotional health of homeschooled students in the United States, a population-based comparison with publicly schooled students based on the National Survey of Children's Health, 2007." *National Home Education Research Institute,* 31. NHERI.org/home-school-researcher-the-social-and-emotional-health-of-homeschooled-students-in-the-united-states-a-population-based-comparison-with-publicly-schooled-students-based-on-the-national-survey-of-child.

Murphy, J. (2012). *"Homeschooling in America: Capturing and assessing the movement."* New York: Corwin Press.

National Center for Education Statistics. (2016). Data on home education. NCES.ed.gov/nhes/data/2016/cbook_pfi_pu.pdf

New York State Education Department. (2019). Part 100 regulations: Home instruction. NYSED.gov/curriculum-instruction/part-100 -regulations-commissioner-education.

Patterson, S. (2019). Unschooling Mom2Mom. UnschoolingMom2 Mom.com.

Ray, B. (2003). "Homeschooling grows up." Home school legal defense association. HSLDA.org/docs/librariesprovider2/public /homeschooling-grows-up.pdf?sfvrsn=69e4f7d1_6.

Ray, B. (2004). *Home educated and now adults: Their community and civic involvement, views about homeschooling, and other traits.* Salem, OR: NHERI Publications.

Ray, B. & Valiente, C. (2020). "The academic and social benefits of homeschooling." JamesGMartin.center/2020/05/the-academic -and-social-benefits-of-homeschooling.

Ricci, C. (2012). *The willed curriculum, unschooling, and self-direction: What do love, trust, respect, care, and compassion have to do with learning?* Canada: Ricci Publishing.

Richards, A. (2019). "Akilah S. Richards (biography)." RaisingFree People.com/about.

Riley, G. (2015). "Differences in levels of competence, autonomy, and relatedness between home educated and traditionally educated young adults." *International Social Science Review*, 2, 1–27.

Riley, G. & Gray, P. (2015). "Grown unschoolers' experiences with higher education and employment: Report II on a survey of 75 unschooled adults." *Other Education*, 4(2), 33–53.

Riley, G. (2018). "A qualitative exploration of individuals who have identified as LGBTQ and who have homeschooled or unschooled." *Other Education*, 7(1), 3–17.

Riley, G. (2020). *Unschooling: Exploring learning beyond the classroom.* New York: Palgrave Macmillan.

Ryan, M. (2009). *Math for Everyday Life.* New York: Grand Central Publishing.

Rudner, L. (1999). "Scholastic achievement and democratic characteristics of homeschooled students in 1998." *Educational Policy Analysis Archives*, 7, 1–33.

Silva, E. (2018, September 21). "The state of homeschooling in America." *Pacific Standard.* PSMag/education/the-state-of-homeschooling-in-america.

Slater-Tate, A. (2016, February 11). "Colleges welcome growing number of homeschooled students." *NBC News.* NBCNews.com/feature/college-game-plan/colleges-welcome-growing-number-homeschooled-students-n520126.

Sorey, K. & Duggan, M. H. (2008). "Homeschoolers entering community colleges." *Journal of College Admission*, 22-28. Files.Eric.ed.gov/fulltext/EJ829457.pdf.

Stright, A. D., Neitzel, C., Sears, K. G., Hoke-Sinex, L. (2001). "Instruction begins in the home: Relations between parental instruction and children's self-regulation in the classroom." *Journal of Educational Psychology,* 93, 456–466.

Tong, S. W. & Tuysuzoglu, I. (2017, December 10). "From homeschool to Harvard. *The Harvard Crimson.*" TheCrimson.com/article/2017 /12/10/homeschool-harvard.

Trotman, D., Lees, H., Willoughby, R. (2017). *Education studies: Key concepts.* London: Routledge.

Vallerand, R., Pelletier, L. G., Koestner, R. (2008). "Reflections on self-determination theory." *Canadian Psychology,* 49(3), 252–262.

Webb, J. (2006). "The outcomes of home-based education: Employment and other issues." *Educational Review,* 41, 121–133.

INDEX

U

Umbrella schools, 54–55
Unit studies method, 45–47
Universal Design for Learning, 28
Unschooling, 25, 34, 41–43

V

Video games, 122–123

W

Well-Trained Mind, The
    (Bauer & Wise), 36
What Your (K–12th) Grader
    Needs to Know series
    (Hirsch), 54
Wise, Jesse, 36

Acknowledgments

To the wonderful Susan Lutfi, and everyone at Callisto Media. Thank you so much for choosing me to write this book. I hope I have made you proud!

To the incredible Jed Bickman. You have been the most fantastic, supportive editor. I feel so honored to have worked with you.

To my colleagues and the administration of Hunter College. You inspire me every single day. Thank you so much for your support of my work. It means more than you will ever know.

The last part of this book was written during a faculty writing retreat at Hunter College, run by Dr. Laura Baecher. So much gratitude to you, Laura, for giving us the virtual space and inspiration to write.

To my graduate students, who mean so much to me. I am in awe of your dedication to the children and teens you teach every single day. Special thanks to Amanda Keningsburg and Zack Stelzner, whose lesson plan ideas show up in this book.

To Dr. Peter Gray, my research mentor and dear friend. Thank you so much for your constant support of my work and for giving me opportunities to do research alongside you. You are a true ambassador of self-directed learning.

To the amazing Howard Blumenthal. I have cherished our brainstorming sessions so much. You are funny and kind and a true champion of authentic learning. I am so grateful our paths have crossed.

To all the homeschoolers who came before me, including those who were involved in Tri-County Homeschoolers in New York during the late 1990s and early 2000s. Twenty years later, I am still so grateful for you all.

To my Bill. Thank you for allowing me the time and space to do the work I love. You are the best husband in the world.

To my beautiful mom, my creative dad, and my wonderful sister, Dr. Bernadette Riley. I am so thankful for all you have done for me. I love you so much.

Finally, to my Ben. I obviously could never have written this book without you. You are my whole heart. I am so very proud of the incredible human you have become.

About the Author

Gina Riley, PhD, is a Clinical Professor and Program Coordinator of the Adolescent Special Education Program at City University of New York—Hunter College. Dr. Riley has extensive experience in online education and distance learning at the college/university level. For the past 22 years, Dr. Riley's research has focused on topics related to homeschooling, unschooling, and intrinsic motivation, an interest stemmed in part from homeschooling her own child from preschool through 12th grade. She is known internationally for her research in the field of self-directed learning.